The
Writer-Photographer

The
Writer-Photographer

JOHN MILTON

CHILTON BOOK COMPANY
Philadelphia · New York · London

Copyright © 1972 by John Milton
First Edition   All Rights Reserved
Published in Philadelphia by Chilton Book Company
and simultaneously in Ontario, Canada,
by Thomas Nelson & Sons, Ltd.
Designed by Cypher Associates, Inc.
Manufactured in the United States of America

Library of Congress Cataloging in Publication Data

Milton, John, 1905-
  The writer-photographer.
  1. Authorship. 2. Photography. I. Title.

PN147.M623   808'.066'07044   72-6305
ISBN 0-8019-5732-X

To all good workmen

The sign that stirred up a story.

COTTONMOUTH COUNTRY

HERE IS THE HOME COUNTRY OF MANY AN EASTERN COTTONMOUTH
THIS VERY POISONOUS SNAKE WONT GO OUT OF HIS WAY EITHER
TO MEET OR AVOID YOU—WILL MORE LIKELY LEAVE THE TRAIL
TO YOU WHILE WATCHING FROM COVER AS YOU PASS. YOU ARE,
HOWEVER, A VISITOR IN HIS HOME, WITH NO RIGHT TO MOLEST
HIM IN ANY WAY.

Preface

"Shortly after I entered Buxton Woods . . . I came upon a path with a sign that said: COTTONMOUTH COUNTRY!"

This is the opening sentence of an article that I wrote for the *New York Times* some years ago. Well, I didn't exactly write it for the *Times*—I wrote it for any publication that would take it. Several nature magazines had a shot at it and returned it, so I filed it away under capital R for Rejections and the piece lay there undisturbed for four full years. Since it was an account of my impressions on discovering for myself the strange jungle-like patch of woods and swamps called Buxton Woods, which is on Hatteras Island off the coast of North Carolina, I gave no thought to the *Times* at all, thinking that it was not their kind of thing.

Then an inspiration was handed to me by my wife who is good at such things. She suggested that I send Buxton Woods to the *Times*, and wound up her reasoning with the words, "Why not?" That did it and I mailed the story on a Thursday. On the following Monday morning my phone rang. It was the editor of the Sunday travel section. He said, in effect, "I'll take the story if you'll send me another couple of hundred words and a picture. Tell the people what a cottonmouth is and how to get there, what the accommodations are and so on. Have you got a picture?" In my surprise and confusion, I said, "I think so"—my spirits drooping a little, for I wasn't a picture-

taker in those days and did not even have a camera. I think that I must have been relying subconsciously on my wife's habit of taking color slides wherever we go. Surely, there must be a slide in her collection that would do. There was. And when the article was published that little color slide was plastered in black and white over five columns, 5½ inches deep. It had saved my story. It looked beautiful. It was my wife's picture, but the credit line was undeservedly mine.

That was the day I should have rushed out and bought a camera, and learned something about photography. But somehow, in my case at least, the most obvious thought sometimes meets an impervious wall in the mind. It registers for the moment, but seems then to be slipped into a pigeon hole reserved for future action. Accordingly, it was months before I did something about it. During that time several experiences with staff photographers of *The Bulletin* in Philadelphia made me realize that not to have and to know how to use a camera was wasting my time and costing me money. Just one instance will serve to illustrate the point.

The editor of *The Bulletin's* Sunday magazine, for whom I had been writing some short pieces, asked if I would write a kind of atmosphere or personality piece about the painter, Andrew Wyeth, whose "friends and neighbors" (numbering more than a thousand) were to honor him at a picnic. Although I had already written my story by the appointed day, the editor asked me to arrange to meet a photographer he was sending to the affair and to show him around so that he could get pictures of the scene and the people for use with the story. If I'd been good with a camera, this would have been unnecessary. I could have been using my day to better advantage; and for that matter, the editor could have saved money for the paper.

My photographic life began with a borrowed picture—a color slide which the *New York Times* published in black and white to illustrate the story about Buxton Woods.

After seven or eight experiences of this sort, I came to know as many different staff photographers, and from my association with them and watching them work I learned a bit about photography as it is used to illustrate articles. The more I looked and listened and learned, the more interested I became in using photography in conjunction with my writing. I bought a camera. It was a Yashicamat twin lens reflex, the same kind used by one of my *Bulletin* friends on standard assignments. When I asked him why he used a rubber band to hold the camera-back in place, he said, "The paper likes to get its money's worth from its equipment. This has been broken for quite a while, but it still takes good pictures."

My camera was brand new. Now that I had added photography to my interest in writing, I wondered how many articles I'd have to write with pictures to match before my camera, too, became a rubber-band wreck.

In actuality, I outlasted that camera rather quickly, having found it not versatile enough to do the work, and turned to a Nikkormat single lens reflex until one day. . . . But that's another story. I now use a Nikon. All three cameras have more than earned their keep and their cost. Ever since the Buxton Woods episode and the few months that followed I have enjoyed the "psychic income" that derives from doing the whole job myself, the satisfaction (as well as the money) that comes from being the writer-photographer.

Acknowledgments

Grateful acknowledgment is given to the following publications for permission to use stories as examples:

The New York Times for FEUD OVER A STRAIGHT-SHOOTIN' RIFLE. © 1966 by the New York Times Company. Reprinted by permission.

The Philadelphia Bulletin for RIDING THE R.D. TRAIL. Reprinted with permission from the Sunday Philadelphia Bulletin Magazine. Copyright, 1964, Bulletin Company.

The Printed Page (The Maple Press) for THE MILL AT LINCHESTER.

Photographs are by the author unless otherwise credited.

Cover photo is by Constance Cozzens Milton.

Contents

Introduction

The writer-photographer is like the man in the band who "doubles in brass"—he plays two instruments equally well. He may prefer one to the other but is competent with both. He may be known as a cornetist (or writer), but be perfectly recognizable behind the trombone (or the camera). What seems to emerge is the image of a man who knows how to make two specialized skills, or talents if you will, pay off for him in terms of satisfaction and money.

This book is directed to the writer who would like to know something about photography so that he can illustrate his stories competently; and it is directed to the photographer who has wished that he knew how to weave words around his pictures. If either of these people is you, it must be said here and now that no special prominence is meant in referring to the writer-photographer. It could just as well be photographer-writer. The result is the same when put together whether one skill is used first or the other.

If you are already a big-name writer you probably wouldn't want to bother with photography, so there is no interest for you here. If you are a photographer whose real interest is salon print making and the winning of blue ribbons, you wouldn't find happiness in fussing with words, too. You couldn't use this book. However, if you fall into either of two much larger groups than those of the pure writer and the pure photographer you can get practical help from this book gleaned from the trial-and-error experience of one writer-photographer who has succeeded in proportion to the effort he put into the work. It remains for the reader to determine what success will come to him. To help guide his feet to that path, it is necessary to mention something of the field itself and of the direction to take.

The field consists of periodicals of one sort or another—magazines of general or special interest, trade magazines of which there are as many as there are business areas and industries, newspapers large enough to have various kinds of departments (travel, garden and the like), Sunday supplements or magazines for local or syndicated consumption, and a phenomenon called the external house organ. These outlets for the work of the writer-photographer are voracious as well as numerous. They eat up material the way television does. The market is always demanding more, and the better your product is the more you will sell.

The one thing to hold in mind here is the writer-photographer combination—the use of the typewriter and the camera as a two-edged tool in the production of income.

From time to time in the chapters that follow, I have found it expedient to draw upon an actual and direct experience which I have used to emphasize or illustrate a point, the real having for me the authenticity in any situation that even the most reasonably constructed synthetic could not possibly provide. These "Case Histories" have practical value as what-to-do or what-not-to-do directives, and since they come from life can be depended upon as help in managing your own progress. I do not intend to inject into a book of this kind anything resembling personal reminiscence as such. Quoted material is from my own work, and when used is designed to serve a practical purpose. The photographs are, in large, mine also, and are selected to help the point being discussed.

JOHN MILTON
Chadds Ford, Pennsylvania

The
Writer-Photographer

1

Writing And Photography– A Matched Team

Writing and photography as they are concerned with producing and selling the whole story for publication go together in much the same way as the words and music of a song join to form the unified whole. Each function can be done as an end in itself, but it takes two people to bring about what one person can do himself. Obviously, it is advantageous to cultivate two skills that are so closely related and so mutually dependent. The person who can do so need have no fear, whether he is a beginner or an already established writer or photographer, that his added skill will be for him less creative or less satisfying than the one he was born to be good at. Both can be as creative as the man using them. If he is a dull writer, he will be a dull photographer, and the other way around, too.

It is plain also that skill in the use of either the typewriter or the camera makes the other more valuable, for one skill alone limits income, not to say satisfaction. A story sold without pictures might bring $100, and with pictures $200. Satisfaction is doubled also.

Consider now why it is that the typewriter and the camera are a natural pair. They are both recording machines that perform the same function in different ways. One uses words as the medium for recording thoughts, ideas, impressions and statements; the other uses film to record the scene, the people, the objects and even the mood prevailing at the time. Used judiciously and with imagination, the two media complement

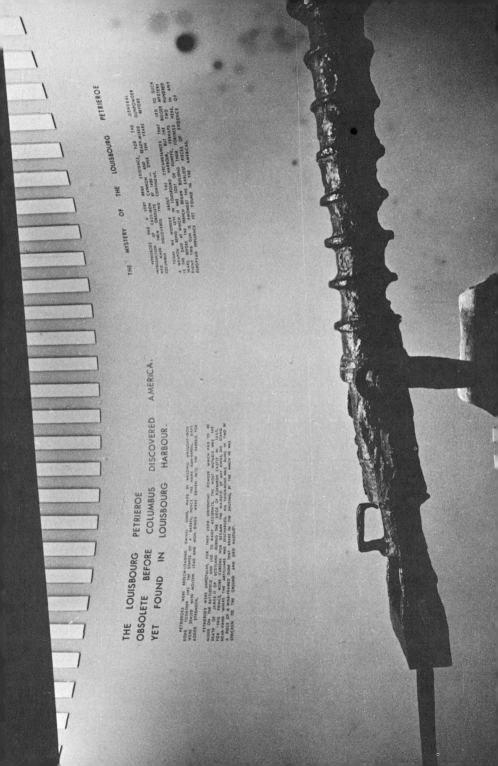

THE LOUISBOURG PETRIEROE
OBSOLETE BEFORE COLUMBUS DISCOVERED AMERICA.
YET FOUND IN LOUISBOURG HARBOUR.

PETRIEROES WERE BREECH-LOADING SWIVEL GUNS, MADE BY WELDING WROUGHT-IRON RODS TOGETHER IN LEADS AND TO MAKE THE BARREL, HENCE THE NAME GUN-BARREL, GUNS WERE SEALED WITH MOLTEN LEAD AND IRON RINGS WERE DRIVEN INTO THE BARREL FOR ADDED STRENGTH.

PETRIEROES WERE UNPOPULAR, FOR THEY USED SERPENTINE POWDER WHICH HAD TO BE MIXED ... THE SHATTERED AND TO MANY ACCIDENTS. THE MOST NOTABLE WAS THE DEATH OF JAMES II OF SCOTLAND, KILLED IN 1460 ... NELL HAND THE PRIEROE, MORE COMMONLY ... THE WEIGHT OF ANY RINGS, DID STAND A PIECE OF A MOSS-FRAMED GUNE THAT BRAKE THE BRICHING, BY THE WHICH HE WAS STRICKEN TO THE GROUND AND DED HASTELY.

THE MYSTERY OF THE LOUISBOURG PETRIEROE

PETRIEROES HAD A VERY BREEF ... EXISTENCE, FOR MIXED INTRODUCTION OF CAST-IRON CANNON AND READY MEDIEVAL THEM OBSOLETE. L'ABO — OVER TEN YEARS BEFORE COLUMBUS DISCOVERED THE CONTINENT. 1848

TODAY WE WONDER ABOUT THE ... LED TO SUCH MYSTERY WEAPON NEAR WHICH IT WAS ... BUT THE BIGGER TWO HUNDRED IS THE PRESENCE IN LOUISBOURG OR ... NEARBY PERHAPS HERE, IN ANY YEARS BEFORE THE FRENCH BEGAN BUILDING THEIR PIECES OF EVIDENCE, OT EVENT THIS GUN IS ONE OF THE EARLIEST ... EUROPEAN INFLUENCE YET FOUND IN THE AMERICAS.

GENERAL GUNPOWDER BEFORE

and embellish each other. They become a well married pair. As such, they present a united front to the reader who, in reading your words and in seeing your pictures, is getting the complete story from a single source and viewpoint. There is never a disparity in the piece when the source and the viewpoint are in harmony; but it can exist when writer and photographer are separate personalities, the writer wanting perhaps to establish a certain mood for his story and the assigned photographer perhaps failing to catch that mood.

One editor with whom I had had a number of dealings in my pre-camera days evidently recognized the possibility of getting the wrong fit of pictures to story—and did something about it. He always gave a copy of the article to the staff photographer assigned to the job so that he could get its drift, and think about it a bit, in advance. On one or two occasions, the photographer of the day, not having a chance to read what we might call his shooting script, spent some time discussing the story with me. They, too, recognized the importance of keying the photographs to the story. As professionals, it was the natural thing for them to do.

In your own handling of typewriter and camera, it is not likely that you will run into staff photographers. This, in a way, is your loss. They work easily but purposefully. They try things that the amateur would never think of. They live sometimes a little dangerously, too. One such instance is worth telling here as a sample of their dedication to getting the picture.

The job was to photograph a small brass cannon, which had been built by a young hobbyist to the scale of the famous Long

A difficult shot taken to record the wording on the circular back wall of a glass display case. My 28mm lens with its great depth-of-field did the job well enough so that an 8 by 10 print showed every word clearly. In reduced size here, the words may not be legible. Note that the words at the left and right are in perfect focus and fade as the wall bends away from the lens. The gun was obsolete ten years before Columbus discovered America, and yet was found in Louisbourg Harbor. How did it get there, and when?

Tom used on naval vessels during the Revolution. None of us standing by was sure that the cannon would hold together. We stood safely away from it. The photographer never gave it a thought. Lying on the ground with his camera a scant three feet from the muzzle and his eye at the viewfinder, he said, "I'll count to three—then let her go." He got the picture.

Quite apart from using the camera to take pictures for your story is another use for it worth special mention. It can copy entire printed pages or handwritten material at the press of a button, and thus give you access to information for later study and use that you would otherwise have to get by laborious and time consuming hand copying. Two notable instances occur to me in which my camera enabled me to get important background facts for use in writing articles. I think they are worth relating for whatever good they might do you in similar circumstances.

I was gathering material for a story on Fortress Louisbourg on the east coast of Nova Scotia which was to be used as an issue of *The Printed Page,* an internal house organ. When you are "on location," as it were, and a thousand miles from your home base, you can't afford to miss anything or to overlook any facts that you might want to use. As a consequence, I was being particularly careful. In the small museum at the Fortress was a glass case standing vertically and containing a printed account of certain historical events. I needed that information and to have copied it by hand would have taken time and several notebook pages. There was some difficulty involved in photographing the words through the glass case because the wording was printed on a circular plane, thus presenting a curved surface to the camera lens. This required a lens with great depth-of-field in order to bring all the words into focus, those at either extreme of the area to be shot being closer to the lens than those at the center. Although conditions were not ideal, a 28mm wide-angle lens did the job with enough definition for me to read all the words when the film frame was enlarged to the equivalent of an 8 by 10 print.

EVENING AND NIGHT SERVICE.

XVI.—ORDER OF EVENING DUTIES.

1. The night service of the large orders of lens lights is performed by two or three keepers, divided into successive watches of four hours' duration, and that of the smaller orders of lenses by one or two keepers, according to circumstances.

2. Every evening, half an hour before sunset, the keepers, provided with a lighting lamp, (lucerne,*) will ascend to the lantern of the tower, if the daily routine has been regularly and faithfully performed, the following will be the condition of things:

a. The lamp of the apparatus, ready for lighting, will be capped with its cover.

b. The clock weight, raised to it greatest height, will be held by an iron rod on a level with the service table.

c. The glass chimney, deposited in a small box or basket, will he placed on the service table, and also the tool-basket containing the ordinary implements of the lighting service.

d. Four glass chimneys and a spare burner fitted with dry wicks must be in reserve in one of the cases of the table of the frame, or in the small closet of the lantern room.

e. In one of the closets of the lantern room must be found the two spare lamps, capped with their covers and fitted with their cords. The one of the two lamps, (which in case of necessity is to be placed in the apparatus,) must, in addition, be fitted with its movable pulley.

f. A vessel filled with filtered oil must be in the lantern room.

g. If there is a revolving machine, the weight will be raised to its greatest height and will be supported by an iron rod; the driving wheel will be held by its clutch, and the bevel wheels will be ungeared.

h. To prevent the failure of a light in the light-house, a taper (lucerne) must be kept lighted in the lantern room, and near by a rod lamp placed ready to be lighted in case it should become necessary to trim or change the service lamp.

i. The curtains of the lantern will be properly spread and hung, and the pieces of the optical parts of the apparatus will be covered with the covers provided to protect them from the action of the sun.

XVII.—TO LIGHT THE LAMP.

a. Everything being in readiness and in order, as presented in XVI, commence lighting the lamp at sunset, so that the light may have its full effect by the time twilight ends.

b. In executing that duty, and in managing the lamp, the following directions must be followed:

c. To light a lamp, commence by raising the wick about one-third of an inch above the top of the burner, and light it at two opposite points, *using for that purpose the small hand-lamp (lucerne) specially designed for lighting, and nothing else.*

d. As soon as the flame commences to rise all around, and before it begins to smoke, lower the wick, and place the chimney in its holder.

---

* Matches, paper lighters, or other means than the small lighting lamps, (lucernes,) must not be employed in lighting lamps.

BODIE ISLAND LIGHTHOUSE
(pronounced "Body")

(Please note: The lighthouse is owned by the Coast Guard, which does not permit the public to enter it.)

At one time there was no Oregon Inlet, but there were inlets opposite Roanoke Island and near New Inlet. The land between was called "Bodie Island" and part of it is still known by that name.

The lighthouse in back of this building still warns seamen of a dangerous coast. One account states that five ships went on shoals within range of the Bodie light while it was being built. It is now automatic, requiring only occasional servicing by Coast-guardsmen. The flashing white 13,000 candle-power light is 156 feet above water, and can be seen 19 miles away.

This Bodie Island lighthouse is the third to be built in the vicinity of Oregon Inlet. The first was undermined by water and sand, and the second was destroyed in the Civil War. Oregon Inlet has moved south more than a mile since the completion of the present lighthouse in 1872.

Another example of note-taking with a camera.

A difficult shot—a photo of a photo taken through an enclosed glass case and enlarged from less than half a frame. This is Diamond Light off Cape Hatteras.

The second instance was similar, yet different. Again it was a matter of shooting through a glass case, this time in a marine museum near Cape Hatteras lighthouse. The document, a copy of which I had to have, was much smaller in size and in the type used, but it was on a nice, flat plane. The light was poor, and since my flash equipment was not at hand (a mistake to be avoided) I tried my fastest lens, an f/1.4 50mm, which I opened wide. The enlarged picture was good enough to give me what I needed.

Thus, the camera is seen to be something more than a producer of illustrations. In the hands of the writer it is also a versatile copying machine that saves time and effort.

2

How To Recognize A Story
When You See One

Probably the one question that every writer or would-be writer has asked at one time or another is, "What can I write about?" And probably the best reply, whether coming from his alter ego in the mirror if the question was asked of himself or from a teacher or counsellor if asked of either of them, was, "Write about what you know." Such an answer is too easy, too pat, too much lacking in specifics—and totally unhelpful. What if you are too young (in years) to have had any kind of varied experience or to have gained any solid knowledge? On the other hand, what if you are a more mature person with some claim to having been around and seen things and acquired some knowledge? In either case would that answer really be of practical help?

I hasten to disabuse you of the notion, if you now have it, that what you know cannot be helpful to you as a writer. Knowledge must be the basis of what you write. However, there is another ingredient that should come first if what you write is to be any good—and that is an interest in the subject you choose, an interest thoroughly spiked by enthusiasm for it. To write about something you know but for which you can generate little interest and enthusiasm is the same as writing a failure—a flop. You won't get any fun out of doing it and no editor will buy it.

There is a way, which has worked for me, to acquire a rich source of story ideas, a source you can tap at will. For want of

Take one skilled carpenter-mason, three years of painstaking work, $30,000 in contributions and tons of enthusiasm—and you can make an old landmark look new. This is the John Chadd House built 250 years ago and now almost restored. Such in-process pictures help to make a good story. The photographer has to follow its progress.

There's a story in these pictures. A cannonball hit this old spring-house at the Battle of the Brandywine in 1777. If you are alert to picture possibilities, as I was in this case, you can get the before- during- and after-restoration shots. Obviously, the during and after shots are less important without the before shot, and you can't get that once restoration has begun.

a better descriptive term, I shall call it The Flycatcher Procedure. It operates on the principle that if the mind is receptive to ideas and is baited with even the slightest touch of imagination it will attract and hold them for later disposal. If you develop expertise in following the procedure you will seldom if ever be without something worthwhile to write about. The question of what to write about disappears.

To recognize a story when you see one demands the uses of imagination, curiosity and the association of ideas. You must give them free play. Success in making them gel hinges on your ability to see things as you look at them. Most people, of course, look at things but few really see them for what they are or suggest. The writer must see—not merely look. Once you look and then see, your curiosity begins to work, your imagination comes into play, and finally thoughts swarm. You find yourself moved into action, spurred on by sharply rising interest and enthusiasm. Here's an example of how it works.

You are walking across a city park. You look at a stray dog wandering aimlessly among the shrubbery, his tail and head lowered, a wisp of rope hanging from his neck. The ordinary passerby looks, too, and makes no mental comment. But you, the writer, see more than the dog. You see him multiplied by a thousand miserable, lonely wretches roaming the city, all of them lost—hungry. Your imagination is fired—your curiosity aroused. You ask yourself how it happens and why. And you wonder what finally happens to these stray animals. You find out about it. You go to the city or county SPCA. You ask your questions and you get answers. The Flycatcher Procedure is working for you—you've got a story. You didn't have it before you entered the park.

Imagination, of course, had a great deal to do with the development of this hypothetical story. I define imagination, for myself, as the extension of what is seen or known or experienced. Curiously, one's imagination seems to be something of a brew or a stew simmering in a pot, for it is almost invariably referred to as something you have that needs occasional stirring.

Pictures that have an association value are always worth taking for possible use. This is something more than an old burned-out building—it is what's left of a famous art studio in Chadds Ford, founded as a school many years ago by Howard Pyle, writer and illustrator, and attended by N. C. Wyeth, Andrew Wyeth and other notable painters and illustrators.

This ancient juniper at the edge of the Grand Canyon gave me the idea for a story about three trees which was used in the *Times*. The picture was taken with a twin lens reflex camera, permitting exceptionally accurate focusing, and good enlargement of detail from the larger film size.

It is, I think, best stirred by the writer when he asks himself questions such as "How can this be used?" or "What is interesting about this?" or "How could this happen?"—all questions that make you wonder about the answers. Accordingly, it appears that imagination can be stirred consciously and deliberately. In this sense, it is a most useful tool—a controlled tool.

Let's have another try at "seeing" a story after "looking" at something. You are in the same park. (Parenthetically speaking, it is Independence Square in Philadelphia, and I know it well,

Lafayette's sycamore shelters his headquarters at Chadds Ford, Pennsylvania.

but it could be one that you know.) You glance idly at the steeple of Independence Hall. You see not a steeple as such but history. You wonder about other historical buildings as represented by their steeples. In less than thirty seconds the processes of your writing mind have developed a story about three famous Revolutionary steeples, all within a few blocks of each other.

PENNSYLVANIA RifLE

Misnamed Kentucky Rifle, this famous weapon of the frontier was developed in the 1700's at Lancaster, which was the center for its manufacture.

The Commonwealth of Pennsylvania claims the Kentucky Rifle as its own at approaches to the City of Lancaster.

(Parenthetically again, I might write this story myself if you don't beat me to it.)

Having mentioned "three" steeples instead of two or four or more, I here pass on to you a bit of lore gleaned from my experience with articles and editors. For some curious reason, editors seem to like three of a kind, and I have more than once fed them what they like. A part of the reason, I suppose, is that two of a kind whet the appetite, and a third thrown in for good measure serves as a comparison for the mental palate to savor. Also, perhaps, the writer himself, in stopping at three, does not mind giving both editor and reader the illusion that if he wanted to he could serve up a dozen, but has carefully chosen three of

Ordinary mile-markers like this can be found at odd places along the line. The opposite side of the marker reads Maryland.

the best. But whatever it is, it seems to work and one might as well go along with it whenever subject and possibility lend themselves to it.

Story ideas can be developed in three distinct ways and the writer-photographer who has learned to be aware of the passing scene and whose eye is observant need never be without a good one to work on. One way occurs by chance; that is, you happen to see something (the stray dog, the steeple) that starts the process going. The second way is deliberately handled or contrived. A third way is, in effect, a combination of the two. With so much going for you in the way of having things to write about, any writer-photographer can find himself with more saleable story ideas than he knows what to do with, beyond putting them into a notebook for future consideration.

In the following case histories, each of the three ways of finding a story is illustrated and is drawn from personal experience.

While at the south rim of the Grand Canyon, I came upon (by chance) an ancient juniper tree that had been clinging desperately to life for hundreds of years. Growing from the bare rimrock, it was contorted and twisted, every branch a grotesque description of hardship. Naturally, I photographed it. That meeting with the tree was pure luck. Before I could leave the place, the association of ideas was occurring and like a flash I realized that I had a story. I recalled two other unique trees that, like this one, had grown up with the country and had "seen" history pass by. Both, however, had had the rich soil of Pennsylvania to support their long lives and had grown handsomely. One is a 500-year-old oak whose branches had sheltered resting travelers between Washington and Philadelphia before the Revolution. The other is a sycamore by the side of General Lafayette's headquarters at Chadds Ford. Now twenty-five feet in circumference at the base, it was a big tree when the Battle of the Brandywine was fought in 1777.

When I returned home and photographed these old giants, I wrote the story and titled it (cleverly, I thought), "America:

Aged in the Wood." *The New York Times* travel section ran it, including four pictures, but the editor thought he saw a better heading for it, calling it "A Toughness of a Kind We Attribute to Our Colonists" which was a quote from the piece itself, so I didn't mind so much.

Thus, you can see how chance operates in seeing and developing a story. If I had not happened upon the juniper, I would probably not have seen the tree story at all, even though I pass by the Lafayette sycamore nearly every day of my life. The juniper sparked it.

The second case history illustrates the cut-and-dried, deliberate attempt to develop a story from a set of facts. In this instance, it is really what you know and what you act on that determine the story—not what you stumble on. I knew from reading the papers that a rifle-shoot was to take place outside of Lancaster, Pennsylvania, between gun buffs who claim that the famous Pennsylvania rifle ("the gun that won the War of Independence") could outshoot what other buffs choose to call the Kentucky Rifle, although the guns are one and the same, having been invented in Pennsylvania and carried by the likes of Boone and Crockett to the west. This merry, little feud is an annual affair, and the shooters in coonskin hats and fringed buckskins have a good and noisy time, as do the spectators. I went there, shot some pictures (although I was invited to shoot a gun), got the story and sold it to the *Times*, the editor titling it, "Feud Over a Straight-Shootin' Rifle."

You can develop stories in this way quite easily by doing a little probing into historical events and dates; for instance, if you know that the Battle of the Brandywine occurred on September 11, 1777 (historical markers tell you this all along U.S. Route 1 in the battlefield area) you can write a story about it and submit it a couple of months in advance of the next anniversary, and in this way give the editor a piece that is timely.

The Information Center at the Peach Bottom Atomic Plant nine miles up the Susquehanna River from U.S. Route 1.

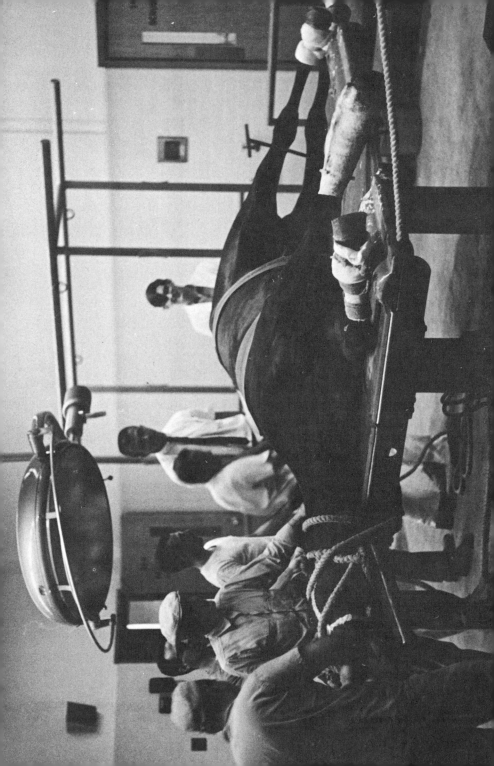

Editors often take kindly to timely stories and the chances of acceptance are then better.

In this connection, a rich source of eventful dates to poke among for ideas is the World Almanac and similar compendiums. I cannot leave this subject without saying that sometimes luck has something to do with your getting a story, as has happened to me, even though the story itself is based on what somebody else knows. I suspect, in my case, that one of the *Times* editors had been browsing through the Almanac, for the editor called me one day and said that he had been told that the 200th anniversary of the establishment of the Mason-Dixon Line was coming up soon. He asked if I could run down there and dig something up for the *Times*. "There" happened to be a scant twenty miles from where I live. I was happy to have the opportunity—an assignment no less. I dug it all right, and it ran as "Line on Mr. Mason and Mr. Dixon." More on this story is to come.

The third case history shows how to work the combination effect to your advantage. This is achieved partly by chance and partly by deliberate choice. You decide to go out to see what you can find. Usually this decision is made when you need a change—when you need to get out of the house and away from your typewriter for a while. The results can be rewarding in several ways.

One morning after several days of intensive work, I felt the need for a mental cold shower, something to stir up new enthusiasm, new interest, new impressions, new something or anything. I went for a ride, taking along with me my camera, a notebook and a sandwich. I did not know where I was going and didn't care, for it seems that chance takes care of things wherever you go. Accordingly, I turned left onto the main road

Illustrating luck with a camera, this picture happened to be there for the taking as I passed by the doorway to the operating room of the veterinary hospital of the University of Pennsylvania at New Bolton, Pennsyvania.

when I might have turned right, and after an hour of easy riding found myself turning onto the long dam that crosses the Susquehanna River at Conowingo, Maryland. Nothing much had attracted my interest until then beyond the normal lure of being in the country on a nice day. I decided that it might be a good idea to visit the power house at the far side of the river and listen to the hum of the generators for a while. After I'd done this, with no particular excitation, I intended to cross the river again and go home by some other road, but a signboard caught my eye and that changed things. It said that the Peach Bottom Atomic Power Plant was nine miles upriver. Those nine miles went up and down through sparsely settled farmland, the last mile angling sharply down to the riverside, and there sat the only atomic plant of its kind in the whole country at the time—a plant cooled by hydrogen.

At the information center I got the story, and I took pictures, but was disappointed in not being permitted to go inside the plant. (Little did the authorities there, or I, know at the time that it wouldn't be long before I'd be given a personal grand tour of the whole marvelous shebang from attic to cellar.) My old standby, the *Times,* published the story, the editor calling it, "Atom Splitter on the Sleepy Susquehanna."

If I had turned right instead of left, I'd have missed the Peach Bottom story; if my eye had not spotted the direction sign, which was small, and if my curiosity had not led me on, I'd have missed it, too. On the other hand, I feel certain that on turning right on the main road something else would have

The photographer's luck holds out—even though the elephant's does not. This circus performer slipped and sprained her ankle (note inflamed right front leg), and became New Bolton's biggest patient. Several days after the picture was taken, the elephant was discharged, but on the way to her home quarters in a truck slipped again, re-injured her leg and had to be destroyed. This picture, with a children's art class at work, added unusual interest to a story about New Bolton.

turned up to intrigue me and pique my interest. The principle
to be followed, however, in this method of developing story
ideas is to make the decision to set out in search of them. Aim-
less though it may seem at the outset to not know where you
are going, the excursion itself is the thing, and what follows
will be the result of the workings of your observant eye, your
curiosity and your ability to see a story when it presents itself.

Sometimes only a borrowed photograph will do the job. These pictures of a small dog on wheels (by Jules Schick) and a big dog on
crutches, you might say (by Sonnee Gotlieb), are from the University of Pennsylvania's newsletter, *Advancing Veterinary Medicine*,
and appeared in the *Philadelphia Bulletin* story along with these of

I'd wager two to one that, all things being equal, any writer can find useful ideas to fill his hopper by following these elementary suggestions.

As a valuable aid in turning up stories apart from the ways already described and illustrated, your camera can take rank equally with your pencil and notebook. Keeping in mind its use as a recording tool, you will find it expedient to take it

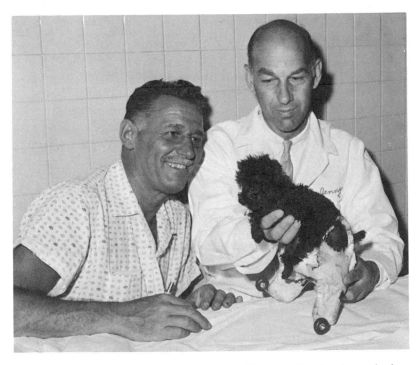

the horse and the elephant. King, the German Shepherd, tracked down and was shot by a murderer in the Pennsylvania mountains; and Missy, the poodle, dislocated her hips and knees, and needed transportation. By the time I wrote the story, both dogs had fully recovered.

with you wherever you go. Sometimes an idle or casual shot of something you see, which at the time has no particular significance in relation to the development of a story, can, on reflection as you see the finished print, suggest a way to weave a story around it. I have in mind an instance in which such a picture turned out rather well and I hung it on my wall with no thought about it other than as decoration. It was a candid portrait of a craggy old man of independent character. As I looked at it one day, it occurred to me that I knew another man with the same qualifications, and soon I recalled a third. I was on my way to a kind of personality story. I would have written it except that one of my characters died before I could get around to getting his picture. But the possibility still remains that I can round out my cast and do the job. Almost every time I look through my print file, I can see other possibilities. I have pictures of chanced-upon wayside auctions, for instance, taken in widely separated parts of the country. They point to a story—and so do pictures of antique shops along the way.

For the writer who holds a steady job and writes as a free-

What writer could fail to find a story—perhaps two stories—based on these pictures of antiques and junk for sale and of a country auction? These scenes were come upon by chance in Maine and in Pennsylvania—the opportunity was recognized, first for picture taking and then as a story—the record was made (the pictures taken)—and when the time is right, the story will be written. These photos and others like them serve me as a backlog of ideas or treasury into which to dip at will. The writer-photographer must remember that in order to have such a reserve of story material he must take his camera along everywhere. Without it, he will never fill up the bin. Each of these pictures has in it something of notable interest—the long line of dishes and empty chairs suggesting that a banquet is simply waiting for the guests to arrive—the crutches for sale—the wheels that suggest a bookmobile—the "Honor Slot" in the door and the picture of Christ—the auction's curious assortment from a grindstone to a baby's ornate crib—and, as we say, a shot from "behind the scenes."

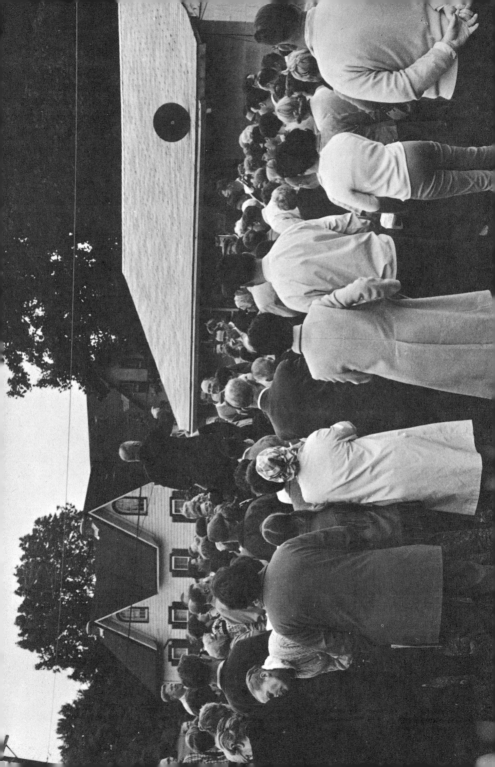

lance using his spare time only, as I do, the time may occur, particularly if he is more or less the beginner, when he has time to use and nothing to use it on. Such times will gradually disappear and then fade forever as he puts to use such help as is presented here. He will in fact find that ideas generate other ideas, and that more likely than not he will be able to acquire a considerable backlog to draw upon as he can.

3

How To Research
The Story And
Gather Material

This is an area of his craft which the writer-photographer must master at the beginning. He will succeed or fail with his articles in proportion to the care, energy and thought expended in getting facts and information on which to draw. How he uses his background material will depend upon his individual ability, but how he collects it in the first place is pretty much a set kind of action and process that is common to every writer with no room left for idiosyncracies or personal vagaries. You can't write an authentic article without having authentic information; nor can you state as the truth what you surmise, or guess, or suspect is the truth.

Accuracy of statement, therefore, becomes the basis of believability on the part of the reader (and we should not forget the editor). Since this is so, it becomes plain that your material must be sound. In support of the necessity to use facts accurately, let it be remembered that the printed word, unlike the spoken word which floats through the air and is forgotten, is irrevocably recorded on paper and filed away in permanent archives. There, your loosely used information and misstatement of fact lie in wait to hound and haunt you.

You will surely hear about your errors of fact almost as soon as the paper or magazine "hits the street"—for there is always at least one reader who knows where you went wrong and who delights in letting the editor know about your failing and his astuteness in picking it up and setting it right. In such case, you, the writer, had better be able to defend your position to both reader and editor, the latter, perhaps, being given preferred attention. Unless you can do so reasonably, it is likely that you will lose more than face with the editor—you will lose his confidence in you as a reliable user of fact, and if that is lost so are sales. The irony of it is that you may be entirely right in every respect but one—that single error, committed carelessly, for which the best course is to admit the fault and offer apology.

When the error is someone else's, as can happen when you use previously printed sources for your facts, or when the publication itself commits a typographical error (in your name) which is serious enough to change your meaning, the fault has to be tracked down and laid at the proper door. After all, why take the blame when it isn't yours? The following three letters concern one of my stories in which a truly funny error occurred, funny now, but not when the first letter arrived with its enclosure. Until I had discovered how the error happened I was disconcerted. The letters speak for themselves.

(Letter to me from the *Times*)

Dear Mr. Milton:
Enclosed is a copy of a letter pertaining to your recent article on the Mason-Dixon Line. I wonder if you would be so kind as to answer Mr. M personally and forward a copy of your reply.

Sincerely
S. D.
Ass't. Travel Editor

(Letter to the *Times* from a reader)

To Travel Editor, New York Times
I'm writing in reference to your article in the Sunday paper of August 20, 1967 on *Line on Mr. Mason and Mr. Dixon* by John Milton.

According to the figures given in the article the (Star Gazer's) stone is located 15 miles east of Cape Henry Light in the Atlantic Ocean.

Very truly yours,
R. P. M.

(Letter from me to the reader with copy to the editor)

Dear Mr. M:

I wish to thank you for pointing out the error in my article on the Mason-Dixon Line. You are quite right! The Star Gazer's Stone is located at 39 degrees, 56 minutes North—certainly not 36 degrees, 56 minutes North as I had it.

When the *Times* sent me your letter, I found myself wondering if I had committed an error in typing or transcribing my copy, but since I have always been careful in this regard, I felt that the mistake must have originated with one of my background sources. As a consequence, I looked into the material I had used, and found where the "36" came from. Since my habit is to use authoritative documentation, I was surprised to learn that the error was in a piece of literature I had found in the (usually very reliable) archives of the Historical Society of Chester County. It is doubtless the only error in the piece, which was written for the Philadelphia Bulletin several years ago by one of that paper's staff feature writers, Mr. H. R. D. It was my luck to have picked up that error! I now wonder whether the Stone is actually 785 feet north of the road sign, as the sign says.

I enclose a photostatic copy of that portion of Mr. D's article in which the error occurred.

Thanks again for writing about the matter. I hope this mistake did not altogether ruin the story for you.

Sincerely,
J. M.

It would have been awkward for me if I had not been able to find the source of the error and to offer proof. Needless to say, the editor's confidence in the accuracy of my work would have been seriously undermined, and my self-confidence sorely tested. There can be no argument about the need to be correct, which, in the writer, is a virtue in its own right, nor about the usefulness of knowing where to lay hands on the source material you have used. Sloppy habits in these areas inevitably lead to unhappiness.

With accuracy ingrained in your consciousness as the prime rule to follow, the next matter of importance is to know the various ways in which you can uncover the information you need. I have found and used five different solid sources on which I have drawn, sometimes singly and sometimes in combination. They are the person or persons interviewed, local historical societies, libraries, personal reference books and, not least, your own detective work. In general, as you approach any of these sources, you do not know what you will turn up; and it, therefore, becomes a great delight when as you dig into them you discover first this interesting piece of information and then that startling fact—just what you needed in more ways than one. Your story is found to have substance—your mind is excited by the prospect of finding still more nuggets—and the story itself seems to be unfolding in your imagination faster than you can jot down facts (unsling your camera and photograph some of them). The effect of all this is a mounting enthusiasm. After all, what on the face of it seemed like a story of sorts is turning out to be something exceptionally worthwhile. But a warning: don't start typing yet—look under all of the stones. Who knows? The unturned stone could yield the key to the as yet unwritten story. First get the facts—then sift them.

In most of the five kinds of sources, you will be dealing with people and asking questions. The way to enlist their help is to come right out with it by telling who you are and why you are there. Anyone who has information that you want (in other words, knows more than you do) will happily spew it up if you ask him if, or express the hope that, he can help you—not will help you—can help you. He invariably can and will. Just as invariably, it is likely that you will have to stop him and put him back on course if he wanders from the subject or concentrates overly on matters of less interest than others. The answers you want will be elicited by the questions you ask.

I have found that the best way, when interviewing someone for a personality piece, is to get the background facts of his life out of the way at the outset—birth date, place of birth, education, family and the like—and then get into what it is that makes him worthy of a feature story. If you don't do this, the chances are that you will omit some pertinent fact which the editor will insist on having, and you then have to backtrack. To point up the importance of this is a little experience of mine. I wrote a story about the artist, Andrew Wyeth. I mentioned his wife and one of his sons. But I neglected to mention his second son. The editor failed to notice it. But—the second son had a girl-friend who didn't let the slight slip by. She wrote me a stinging letter, accusing me of "even mentioning Mr. Wyeth's dog"— which I had not done at all.

After getting the personal facts out of the way, the wise course, it seems to me, is to let the subject do the talking, as your questions serve as a prod to guide him this way and that. Usually, something like, "What happened then?" or "Why do you do it that way?" will draw him out; and when subject and interviewer have settled down to a friendly basis, the interview generally becomes not a cold question and answer affair but an intimate discussion—two friends talking together—the best way for the writer to "get inside" his man and to come away from the meeting with a valid feeling for him and about him. Your impression of him as you write his story will be the making of it. If you can generate a sympathy, an understanding, a oneness with him—it will show up in your writing as enthusiasm, properly restrained. Considered as an attitude in your writing, such enthusiasm will generate a like feeling in the reader.

The question may arise in your mind—"Why not use a recorder when interviewing instead of relying on impressions and notes?" My answer to this is that something is lost in the transcription, something very valuable. Spontaneity and sparkle have gone. Inhibition sets in on the part of the subject whose eyes dart to the machine and whose mind is concerned with how he is saying it—not with what he is saying. The interview becomes cold, as does the result. The recorder intrudes between the subject and the writer. Far better, it seems to me, is to write from deeply felt impressions gained without strain from friendly, unselfconscious conversation. In this way, the story becomes a true account to which the reader is naturally attracted.

I was once asked by an editor to interview an 81-year-old man and was told that I was to look up a friend who would introduce me. The friend warned me that the old man was unpredictable and might or might not "take to" me. "All I can do," he said, "is to take you there and tell him who you are." He did so and left. In three minutes, the old man and I were talking together at a great rate, all because I think he felt my genuine desire to be a friend. I hate to think of what might have happened if I'd asked him to sit there and talk into a microphone.

When the subject is not an individual, but a place, a building, an object or objects, the search for facts is still likely to depend upon what an individual can do for you, through both what he tells you and what he can give you in the way of printed material concerning the subject. Here is a good example.

The subject was a house built in 1704 which had been brought back to its original condition after having been neglected for many years. When I went there, it was closed to visitors, and I might simply have taken pictures and gone away; but I noticed that a small outbuilding seemed to be occupied, so I knocked on the door. A pleasant woman opened it and I told her who I was and what I had hoped to do—write a piece about the old house. With that, she brightened as though I had brought her a gift, which in a sense I had, for in giving her the opportunity to tell me about it I had touched upon her own interests and enthusiasms. As caretaker for the place, she could indulge in what had become for her a hobby rather than a duty. She fetched a key and for the next two hours fed me the story in digestible bits. Further, she went to lengths to give me a printed set of historical facts, and finally loaned me a rare old photo-

graph to copy on the promise that I would return it. My own camera at work inside the house turned out some good shots of rooms, fireplaces and pre-colonial objects and furnishings. It was a good day and a successful story.

With respect to printed pieces as a source of information, I formed the habit early of collecting such material wherever I travel. Although much of it might never be used, I do not know this at the time; but when it is needed and is at hand it is invaluable. I have relied on it and used it time and again. Much of this material is free for the asking—maps, local history, points of interest, historic sites, what to see—and as much is to be bought and is worth buying—pamphlets and booklets, art catalogues, books of special or local nature. It is all grist to the writer-photographer's mill, and grind out of it what you can. Just keep in mind that if you don't get it when you are there you won't have it when you want it.

It is often the case that one subject-idea picked up in such literature leads directly to another. I recall that seven or eight years ago, while "doing" an issue of *The Printed Page* on the colonial iron forge at Hopewell, Pennsylvania, a mention was made in a folder about Hopewell that another important early forge was located at Cornwall in the same general area. That fact came to my notice only a year ago as I was browsing through the old Hopewell material, and I produced a piece about Cornwall which included twenty photographs.

Another in my list of sources to be depended upon for valued information is one of the most obvious—libraries and librarians. When you consider that all of Man's information is recorded somewhere in books and that libraries are where the books are, you know where to go to lay your hands on material, ranging from a pamphlet or monograph to a tome, needed to give you

The Brinton House, built in 1704, is surrounded by trees, making a picture of the house itself difficult to get. A 28mm lens enabled me to get inside the trees for a full shot of the gable end including the tall chimney.

background and specifics on your subject of interest. Libraries range, of course, from the small-town variety (probably Carnegie-endowed) through the college and university and the big-city kinds to the king of them all, the Library of Congress. The beauty of it is that all are open to your investigation, and are likely to be manned by the kind of people who feel that they would be remiss in their duty if they did not try to help you find what you are looking for.

I categorically love all librarians because I have never found one yet who failed to express interest in trying to help. You should use their services. They take pride in coming up with what you're after.

I think it expedient here to lump in with libraries a sort of auxiliary which can be of prime importance in your arsenal of sources. I refer to newspaper files, particularly those maintained by the large papers. For many years, the metropolitan dailies (and many libraries, too) have been reducing each day's paper to microfilm. By consulting an index, you can locate the item you would like to see and read it enlarged from the microfilm. You can buy a copy of the item. Some papers even have a mail order service which provides such copies for those not able to visit the paper in person. You can obtain a news account of a disaster (the burning of the zeppelin Hindenburg at Lakehurst, New Jersey, for example), or an obituary of a world figure, or a notable editorial, or whatever item of information you need for your writing. Like the library, the large newspaper is by its very nature a treasury of facts. The phrase, "As dead as yesterday's newspaper," to the contrary notwithstanding, the newspaper of today, yesterday and the day before is a living record that is dead and buried only for those who do not know how to make use of it.

The third source on which I depend for material is local or county or state historical societies and their archives. The first two are something of a phenomenon, I think, because their membership consists of people who are history buffs, particularly with reference to anything having to do with their geographic area—their home grounds, so to speak. As such, they go out of their way to help anyone (particularly a writer) who shows interest in their territory and what it has to offer. These societies collect and display historical artifacts which can be seen and photographed but not always touched or handled; they collect and catalogue everything of some note that has ever been written about the locale or county; they file this wealth of material away and are able to resurrect it for examination without delay or fuss. In fact, at society headquarters the people on duty take the same pride as the librarian does in giving the researcher material he can use; and sometimes they go to unusual lengths to make things possible.

I recall, for instance, when I was trying to find information for the article on the Mason-Dixon Line, that I went to the Chester County Historical Society in West Chester, Pennsylvania, in the hope that I could find something good and basic to help me along. Before I left there an hour later I had two enormously important elements of my story—a photograph and a road direction to follow. With these, the rest was easy. The society member who was helping me gave me a batch of clippings to look over, then said, "And we have a picture of a crownstone." A crownstone was set into the ground to mark five-mile intervals of the Mason-Dixon Line. On one side of these granite posts, which had been brought from England and lugged into the wilderness by hand and horsepower, the crown or arms of Maryland was carved, and on the other, of Pennsylvania. Although a few crownstones still remain where they were set more than 200 years ago, they are difficult to find because the Line runs through woods and fields inconveniently far from traveled roads. I was elated to have a picture of one. "Oh, no! You can't have the picture. We don't know where it came from and it is the only one we have." I asked for permission to rush it out to a photofinisher to make a copy. "No, we can't let it leave the building." I asked if I could photograph it myself just outside of the building in the sunlight. "Yes, if you can manage it in the alley through this side door." I needed some-

Rare picture of a Mason-Dixon Line crownstone was borrowed, set up on an antique chair and photographed.

thing to prop the picture up on. "Take this chair with the spindle back, but be careful with it." It was an antique.

The road direction given by the Society lady led me, after careful navigation, to the edge of a cornfield a few miles out into the countryside. I climbed a steep bank to reach the field, and there was my second find of the day, the "Star Gazer's Stone," which had been placed there in 1764 by Mason and Dixon who were trained astronomers, hence Star Gazers. This was their reference point 31 miles west of Philadelphia from which they then surveyed their way southward to the border of Maryland. The quality of this story was good and became so by virtue of the exceptional help given me by the Historical Society.

What the Society asked for in return was a copy of the article when published (the lady had kindly refrained from saying "if published").

I cannot imagine any writer of consequence being without certain kinds of books which, in effect, constitute his personal branch library. Here is a fourth source of facts to be relied upon—a source that is the more valuable because it is right there, at your elbow, ready to be consulted for the word whose meaning you are unsure of, for the date or proper name that eludes you, for the correct quotation, for whatever it is that you need at the moment to keep your writing going accurately. It is always bothersome when writing to have to stop for want of a fact, to make a list of what you need to know, and to make a trip to the library to get the answers. You can lessen or prevent this kind of obstruction by having at hand at least some of the basic sourcebooks—dictionary, encyclopaedia, atlas, gazetteer, Bartlett's Quotations—and the more the merrier.

It seems superfluous to mention that you must have a good dictionary at the beginning, if nothing else. Other reference books can be picked up at second-hand bookstores as you run across them. The main thing is to collect them at every opportunity. My own collecting (I should say "our" collecting, for my wife, too, is an avid gatherer of literary sources) has resulted in a number of dictionaries of various kinds ranging from the usual good desk volume to the big Oxford Universal model. American editions, English editions, and editions that feature foreign language comparisons or other specialized areas of information are among them.

An encyclopaedia is of next importance, the one I use most being the handy, one-volume *Columbia Encyclopaedia*. Other necessary reference books must include at least a biographical dictionary and, of course, the highly useful *World Almanac*. Although I have already mentioned Bartlett's Quotations, whose title is more properly *Familiar Quotations*, I emphasize the need to have a copy in the house. Apart from its usefulness in looking up a quotation for its intrinsic interest, you will find it priceless when trying to find a peg to hang the story on, a device which will be explained in a later chapter.

It can be said in general that the more you develop your own collection of source materials, the more you will be able not only to come up with useful ideas but also to check out your facts in the quickest way. Start with the basic sourcebooks, and add them as you find items that appear to be useful.

The fifth method of gathering information depends upon your own ability and initiative to track down from a slight lead the facts that might make a story—in other words, your own detective work. Of course, when the lead presents itself, you must be able to determine whether or not it has possibilities. I can best describe how this works by relating a case history, step by step, as it occurred.

While I was talking with a man who had just delivered a bag of salt for use in the water conditioner in my basement, he mentioned having seen a feature I had written which had appeared in the Sunday magazine of *The Philadelphia Bulletin*. Then he

Final print of the crownstone was made from that portion of the negative which did not show the spindles and seat of the chair. Detail was maintained despite enlargement from such a small area of the negative.

said, "I know where there's a good story for you if you can find the guy. He makes cannons in his cellar. The trouble is—I don't know his name or where he lives, but I do know that it's somewhere in this corner of the county. I heard about him somewhere." I was all ears. The idea sounded good, but all I had to do was to find the man who had no name and no address. The impression given to me was that the cannon-maker was some sort of machinist who had a job and worked on his hobby in his spare time. On the following morning, I set out to find him.

"This corner of the county" is a large rural area having several small towns along U.S. Route 1 which runs through it. My informant's home base was in one of them, so that's where I started looking. I went to the post office and asked a clerk if she knew of a man who made cannons. She turned and broadcast my question to several mailmen who were sorting mail at the back of the room. I had hit the jackpot. One of the men said, "You must mean George Johnson (which is not the real name). Go down Smith Road (also fictitious) for two and a half miles, then look for three dirt lanes on the left side. The third lane leads to Johnson's place." I set the odometer in the car to zero and started out. But I found no dirt lanes at all and after going five miles turned back. At the two and a half mile spot, I turned around and tried again. I found three lanes but they were all paved. Plainly, the mailman had not known that the dirt lanes had all been recently paved. I tried the third lane, and soon found that it was leading me between a long, curving line of trees to what appeared to be a country club. Figuring that I was on the wrong track again but that someone at the club might be able to help, I continued until I reached a row of garages under the building. Two young men were fussing with one of the cars. One of them was George Johnson.

My conception of the cannon-maker as a grubby machinist working hard for extra money was in error. Actually, he was a machinist when he was making cannons, and he did work hard; but he was also several other things—a millionaire's son, an Ivy League graduate summa cum laude, a candidate for the Ph.D. in International Finance at Johns Hopkins University, an explorer of the Amazon, the holder of a private plane license and the co-author of a book on finance. He sold his cannons, at $300 each, to yacht clubs mostly, so that they could fire off a "noonday gun" to signify that the sun was over the yardarm or maybe to signal the start of yacht races.

It all made a good story and it came through a chance remark made by a man who had happened to read an article of mine. But it might not have developed at all if I had not recognized a story in the information given and if I had not scouted around asking questions. That's all it takes—looking around, asking simple questions and adding two and two. The same formula has led me to some stories and to even more story ideas, for often the people you talk to offer suggestions, some good, some bad, but all worth giving a moment's thought to.

Regardless of how you go about collecting information or where you get it, a main point to keep in mind is to be thorough about it. This should include the way you record facts as someone is giving them to you. Unless you know shorthand (which I don't) you will find yourself running far behind your man if you try to write every word down, and you will be stopping him constantly and saying, "What was that you said?" I have solved this problem successfully by jotting down key words only and relying on memory to fill in. It is truly amazing to me when I see my notes some time later and am able to recall what was said. The key words have no meaning for anyone else —they give me the story. How I feel about the individual—his manner, appearance and surroundings—provides a powerful impetus for the writing. Of course, impressions of a place or scene or object compounded of what you know of its history and fired by a touch of imagination can do the same thing.

In your search for material, it is important when approaching a person, whether the subject himself or someone who might help you, to represent yourself honestly. You are a writer who is interested in writing an article about this or that subject. You are asking for help. Unless you have the article all sewed up in advance with the publication, it is wrong to intimate, much less to say, that you are *from* the publication or that you are writing it *for* the publication. You can get into trouble that way.

I had the greatest difficulty one time, even though I had the

It's not all work and no play with the cannon-maker. Here, his Long Tom is set up to fire upon and sink a ship model floating in the pond.

assignment from *The New York Times*, with a man who was to introduce me to several people. He kept saying that I was from the *Times*, or referring to me as the *Times* man. I finally had to draw him aside and say, "Look, I am a freelance writer. I don't work for the paper. It just happens that the editor asked me to get this story." In this instance, although I was actually a pro tem *Times* man, my concern was that the editor might hear that I was representing myself falsely, and I couldn't afford to lose the editor's confidence. It is curious to note despite what I have just said that any freelance writer who contributes to this paper is given an employee number which appears on each check voucher—so maybe I *was* employed by the *Times* now and then.

Nonetheless, it is best to represent yourself accurately.

4

How To Get
The Pictures You Need

Since pictures are a part of the material that you need in preparing to write a story or article, it follows that the thoroughness with which you collect information should apply to your picture taking, also. It is good common sense, as well as good business, to go about getting pictures as though you had but one chance to do so. This is the case in most instances, as when, for instance, you are a long distance from home and to go back for more pictures would not be economical. Of course, there is the inevitable exception—the time when the need is clear and it is both possible and practical to go back for more. Such a time occurred when I was photographing for the Cornwall Furnace piece, mentioned earlier. I was there first in winter. The interior shots were made in a cold, dank atmosphere, for the building was unheated and the thick, stone walls added nothing to comfort. I remember fumbling clumsily as I hurried to slip a new roll of film into the camera. So the pictures were not altogether to my liking. Also, the trees were bare and the general bleakness of the scene detracted from the natural beauty of the setting. So I went back in the spring and did the job over again, traveling 150 miles.

It is wise to do it right the first time for another good reason. What you see before you when you are there exists, whether it is a scene, a person or an object. Your subject of the moment may have changed radically or disappeared entirely the next time around.

For equally good reasons, the smart thing to do when photographing is to take more shots than you are likely to use for the story you have in mind. An editor generally likes to see a half dozen photographs if the publication is a newspaper or magazine, and perhaps twenty or more in the case of a house publication. Since you have to give him enough to choose from, you must not be stingy with your film, which is cheap

The only operating up-and-down, water-powered saw left in the country—Menges Mills, Pennsylvania.

No one knows how many millstones have been retired in the 233-year history of Menges Mills.

when balanced against the possible return to you. So shoot away, and shoot often. Perhaps you'll be more inclined to do that when you realize that what the editor does not choose might be used by you in connection with some other story.

The day is fresh in my mind when I received from an editor, to whom I had sent six pictures, a package containing the three rejected ones. I was amazed and disappointed to see that he had returned the one photo that I had counted on him to use. I would have bet on it. A month later I was glad

The mile-long mill race was dug by hand.

that he had chosen as he did, for since the picture was now mine and not the property of the publication, I was able to use it as the lead photo in a 16-page booklet. On other occasions, my photo file of unused or rejected photographs has turned up shots that made their way into print elsewhere. The only way you can go wrong in taking plenty of pictures is to take multiple shots from the same or virtually the same viewpoint. What you need is variety.

Let us say that you are writing a story about an old gristmill. To cover it photographically, you should get shots of the exterior from all sides. Get the approach to it from a distance with the mill in the background. Get a shot from the inside looking out a door or window. Get close-ups of interesting details of doorway, threshold, millwheel, millstones (grinding stones), handtools. Get the millrace and the water tumbling from the wheel. Get the miller, himself, if there is one. Get the oak pegs that have held the old place together for so long. By the time you are through, you will have used from forty to sixty frames, or from two to three rolls of film. Don't be

Stone threshold at Menges Mills worn down by tread of many feet —an interesting photographic detail.

afraid of using film—count opportunities, not pennies (anyway, it's tax deductible).

I've taken pictures of several such mills, and of all those pictures one in particular tells a unique story. It is a picture of a hole—a hole at the bottom of a door. The miller of a hundred years ago made that hole in his bedroom door (millers slept in) to accommodate the comings and goings of his cat. Such details make good pictures. Don't overlook them. Another story-telling detail in the same mill is shown in a photograph of the granite threshold, worn several inches deep by another kind of coming and going—the steps of farmers bringing grain to the mill and taking flour away.

If the subject is a person, rather than a structure, your photography will follow a different line. You will want a couple of posed portrait shots, of course, but perhaps of greater importance and interest will be those you will get of the subject in his relaxed moments—the candid shots that tend more to reveal him as he really is. To achieve this is not particularly difficult, but it is dependent upon the rapport between you, the photographer, and him, the subject. The best advice based on my experience is not to go banging away the moment you arrive but to wait a bit and depend upon a little conversation to soften the way. Your subject knows why you are there and he knows what a camera is, so, since he is not averse to the idea of being photographed the time is bound to come when the atmosphere is relaxed and friendly. Get your straight (posed) portraits out of the way; then, as you talk in general, you can move about a bit and shoot your man from various angles without disturbing the mood or, for that matter, interfering with the talk. The subject is likely to overlook entirely the fact that he is being photographed. These are the most

A typical contact sheet or print showing all of the pictures on a 20-frame roll of film, making it easy to pick-and-choose frames for enlargement. In this instance, it was possible to squeeze 21 pictures out of the roll.

interesting pictures, and after you've tried a session or two of this kind of work, you'll have the hang of it.

While you are shooting is not, of course, the time to think of or consider what pictures to submit with your story. That time comes when you have prints to examine and select from. The best way to do this is to have your photo finisher make a contact sheet. This is a single sheet of photographic printing paper on which each of the pictures on a roll of film is printed in contact size, or the exact size of the film frame. In other words, if your roll of film takes twenty pictures, all of them would be printed on the same sheet, which would be about 8 by 10 inches. Since the contact sheet shows you what is on the entire roll, you can pick and choose the frames you want to enlarge without shuffling individual pictures around. If you use a magnifying glass when examining the contact pictures, you will get a much better idea of their value as enlargements, and will also be able to compare their quality on the basis of definition.

Let us assume that you have before you such a contact sheet. You study each frame under the glass, and reject or accept it. You finally decide on six pictures as the best to show your subject in a variety of ways. Since each frame has its own number, you list the six numbers, and have the chosen frames enlarged by your photofinisher. This leaves you with fourteen (temporarily) rejected frames, some of which you might make use of at another time. If, instead of using the contact sheet method of picture selection, you had before you the small, wallet-size prints that come back from the photofinisher as a regular thing, you would have spent more money than necessary. To enlarge the twenty frames even to wallet-size costs more than to make a contact sheet—about three times more. Thus, the contact sheet method is both cheaper and more convenient.

Sometimes a photographer, with his contact sheet before him, can be heard to mutter, "Why the deuce didn't I bracket that shot?" You can avoid having to ask yourself that question by knowing what bracketing is and when it is wise to do it. It's all simple enough. To bracket a shot means to take a picture at a certain exposure, and then to take a shot at a value immediately above that exposure and one immediately below it. It is done when you are not sure that your exposure setting is right and you are, in effect, taking a guess at it. For example, if you figure that your camera setting should be at f/8 and the shutter speed at 125, you would shoot the picture at these values. Then, to make sure, you would shoot the same subject using the f/ stops next to f/8; i.e., one shot at f/11 and one at f/5.6. You are letting three different light values affect the film, one below and one above the value you think is right. Thus, you bracket the shots. The same thing can be done by leaving the f/ stop alone after choosing it in the first place and by using different shutter speeds, the first shot at 125, then one at 250 and another at 60.

The need to bracket a shot arises from time to time and for various reasons—you might have left your light meter at home, your built-in light meter has run out of battery power, the light is such that in viewing the subject through your viewfinder you cannot see the exposure needle or indicator. So you guess at the settings and take a chance. Then you increase the chances by bracketing. It's another way of getting the picture.

It should go without saying that the photographer should be prepared to handle any photographic situation that he runs into. Thus, to know in advance what sort of conditions might be encountered is a safety measure to be relied upon in the prevention of trouble. For instance, when you realize that film costs more in out-of-the-way places, you will make sure that you have plenty of it in your bag. For some strange reason, every photographer in the world has run out of film at one time or another, just as every automobile driver has run out of gas. Perhaps it is a human trait working in both connections which permits us to believe that there's always a supply of what we want just around the next bend. If you hold this belief, I feel duty compelled to disabuse you of the notion as quickly and as firmly as possible. *It is not so.* Those four monosyllables hold the whole truth. I urge you to carry enough film with you to shoot twice as many pictures as you expect to . . . maybe three times. I follow my own preaching now, but there was a time when I went on the "next bend" theory. Once it cost me money. That was in British Columbia where a roll of film was priced three times higher than at home. And once it cost me time and convenience. That was at Cornwall Furnace where the nearest supply was three miles away, requiring that I pack up my equipment (you never leave it with anybody), make the trip, and then set up and work again.

You should not find yourself in the position of needing a filter or a flashgun or a different lens only to realize that you left it at the foot of the mountain in the car while you are at the top. As has been said, you can't go back—so take with you what you will surely need and consider, too, what might come in handy. This does not mean that everything you own has to go along. Reason has to be your guide . . . and the laws of probability. You'll learn.

There are other safety measures that can be taken to make it possible for you to get the pictures you need. One of these may seem to you, on first consideration, to be somewhat extreme . . . have a backup camera. Have two cameras. What a luxury! you say. It's like having two cars in the garage when I'm the only driver in the house. I can't use them both at once. And besides, with my expensive new camera how can I afford another?

All right, say it. Then please forget your shock, if not your indignation, and listen to reason. Two cameras make sense. Your first or prime camera should be the best you can afford (if you do right by it, it will pay for itself). The second camera could be the one you kept because they wouldn't give you anything much for it as a trade-in, or the one your wife uses now and then to take color slides, or an inexpensive new or used automatic that uses drop-in cartridges. But, no matter how you acquire one, there is one overriding good reason for having it . . . if the No. 1 camera fails, the second will do in a pinch.

My wife and I set out one Sunday morning after a new fallen snow to get some pictures of the countryside. I composed a scene through the viewfinder and pressed the button. Everything I was looking at turned black. The flip-up mirror in the camera body had come loose and jammed the mechanism. If the occasion had been important to a story, I would have been in trouble. But it wasn't and I wasn't. My wife got the pictures that day, and if I had needed black and whites I could have gotten them from her color slides.

However, on another day I was working, taking pictures of a colonial mansion in Odessa, Delaware. I used up two rolls and went home. At that time, I was using the darkroom skills of a friend of mine instead of the services of a commercial photofinisher. When he made contact sheets of both rolls, it was found that about half of the exposures on both rolls were far too dense, or overexposed. Since I knew that photographic conditions were ideal when the shots were taken, the fault had to be in the camera. We tested the shutter speeds and found that half the time the shutter was working fine, and the other half its action was sluggish, causing too much light to reach the film. That camera went to the shop for six weeks. But I had a backup camera by then and wasn't out of business. Fortunately, enough good pictures came out of those rolls to care for the job I was working on. A number of literary figures (writers is a better word), among them Churchill, Fielding, Butler, and Chapman, have referred to the wisdom of having "two strings" to your bow—a lesson good enough for the writer-photographer to put to use.

A second camera has another value in addition to that of safety. Load it with color film, instead of letting it lie around idle, and you'll be ready to get that occasional, rare shot that is at its best in color. Then, if No. 1 breaks down, you will still come home with something to show.

Photographers who work at it every day often have two camera bodies of the same make and interchangeable lenses.

One camera is loaded with monochrome (black and white) film, the other with color. In this case, only one set of lenses is necessary, which, of course, is a great saving. If the camera bodies were of different makes and the lenses of one did not fit the other, two sets of lenses would be required. A second camera body of the same make as your first camera can often be bought reasonably at a good camera shop.

In getting the pictures you need, one of the best and most valuable aids is a friend who knows how to use a darkroom and who is happy to do your photofinishing at cost—or for that matter, at a profit. I have such a friend—and my advice to you is to find one as quickly as possible. I won't tell you my friend's name—he's mine. You'll have to find one for yourself. To do that is not as difficult as it sounds. Join your local club of amateur photographers (there's one in every area)—find some compatible soul there whose hobby is his darkroom—worm your way into his confidence—and latch on to him.

Such a friend can do wonders with your (sometimes) mediocre or poor negatives, using his enlarger and dodging arts to coax good pictures out of them. At the commercial photofinishers, the same negatives would yield nothing. My friend has enlarged an area the size of your little fingernail, taken from the center of the frame itself, which is only 1 by 1½ inches, to a 5 by 7 print that was good enough to be accepted for publication. This is something that only an expensive custom photofinisher would tackle, and that the regular commercial place would not even touch.

When the shutter failed that day in Delaware, my darkroom friend saved a number of overexposed pictures by careful dodging during the enlarging process. Dodging, by the way, is a method of regulating or controlling the amount of light reaching the printing paper by means of a flat object interposed between the negative and the paper and moved in a circular motion. It requires a deft hand and artistic judgment. Only a friend would put out this way to help you along with your pictures.

Occasionally, you might have to put friendship to the test.

It usually happens like this: the editor calls and asks if you could possibly get an entirely new picture to him within 24 hours, and since the subject is only 10 miles away, you say sure; your camera is already loaded with fresh film (naturally) and you take the picture and then shoot one more for good measure; you rush to your friend's house with the film and look into his eyes as you wear a quizzical expression on your face and shrug your shoulders, as though to say, "I'm stuck—I can't help it"; he seizes the film without a word and turns to the darkroom where he develops the negative and prints the two pictures, throwing the 18 unused frames away; you rush the pictures to the post office; and then you realize what a good friend you have.

Please note here that to get what the editor wanted it was necessary to waste most of the film. Two shots were taken, 18 frames were not used. There is no way to prevent such waste when a fresh film is used and only one picture is needed, unless your camera takes sheet film. However, the likelihood is that your camera takes roll film, as 99 out of 100 do, and therefore, you might have to waste a frame or two now and then in order to get a particular picture out of the camera in a hurry. When you have a choice of doing the expedient thing or the wasteful, the professionalism in you will dictate the former. I know people, as you undoubtedly do, who break out their cameras once in a while and take a rash of pictures all in a day. Then with 18 exposed frames in their cameras screaming to get out and be looked at, they put the cameras away until the mood strikes again, because there are two unused frames. A frame costs about 3¾ cents.

In the professional view, getting the picture is all that matters. You should not infer that professionals deliberately waste film or any other material that they have to buy and pay for. What they do is to make use of it wisely, and they place one value against another before making decisions. Thus, sometimes it pays them to waste a few frames. Sometimes, too, they make up for these frames by squeezing an extra picture out of a normal 20-frame roll.

5

Writing The Story

It has been said many times that writing cannot be taught. What is meant, I think, is that the aptitude for writing cannot be taught. The true writer has a deep-rooted writing urge that stems from an inherent affinity for words, their meanings and their uses in disciplined sentence construction. He can be guided and advised, and his work can be constructively criticized by an instructor. But he learns his art or his craft by using it. He already owns the tools. As his experience grows, he becomes a sort of literary ringmaster who is in complete control of his charges—the words of his language—and he can make them run and leap and dance, or slow to a pedestrian pace, according to the mood he wishes to establish in the piece he is writing. The true writer uses the correct word to express an exact meaning, and yet he understands the nuances of words and their imagery and how to wring from them all the subtlety and allusiveness afforded by them. Because he is so basically grounded in the "rules of the road" he can deliberately break them on occasion for the purpose of tempering or leavening the tone of his writing. To be rigidly correct and stiffly proper at all times is not the end in view. The musician deliberately uses the off-beat for its effect; the writer does the same. Out of his writing, the writer develops a style—his way of writing—which is simply an extension of his inner characteristics. For instance, if a man's personality is essentially serious, his writing is not likely to show the saving grace of a touch of humor. Thus, a writing style is a mark of the writer himself.

Clarity should be the principal aim in writing—a clarity of expression which transmits thought from the writer's mind to that of the reader without loss in transmission—without static, if you will. This can best be achieved if the writer's thought is clear, if he then uses the proper words in orderly succession, and if he avoids unnecessary, useless or superfluous words which detract from the main message. Obviously, no writer intends to write obscurely in order to be obscure. When his thought is obscure, his writing will have the same fault.

To write plainly, then, would appear to be a virtue—and so it is; but unless the plainness is relieved by the writer's ability to touch his sentences with the salt and pepper of imagery, the writing becomes dull and the shine rubs off. Who reads a dull writer?

People read articles for the amusement or entertainment value in them, or because the subject is of particular interest at the moment, or because the information given is useful. To supply one or more of these values requires that the writer pay some attention at the outset to both the subject he is writing about and the kind or class of reader likely to be involved. The idea is to get the story and the reader together in harmony. If your article is about the rough, tough life of the sandhog, you would scarcely expect that the readers of a magazine published by The Ladies Wednesday Evening Sewing Circle of America would get much of a bang out of it. Nor would the readers of *Jack and Jill* be enthralled by your account of a meeting with the world's greatest philosopher. However, if you're doing a piece on a new metallurgical alloy, you would be right in directing it to a trade magazine serving the industry involved.

Readers of a given publication tend to have interests in common. In your mind's eye, then, you can summon up a kind of composite reader as you write, and in writing to this more or less real person can achieve the sincerity and closeness of a one-to-one relationship. The reader will feel that you are writing for him alone.

Accordingly, you write most successfully when, depending on subject, you write for a specific class of reader, and in a tone or at a level designed to be understandable to that reader. In doing so, you must not commit the fatal error—the killing of interest in your story—which occurs when you write below the intelligence of your readership. That intelligence can be surprisingly high, and it is better to write up to it than below it.

When you have before you all of your background material, your photographs and your notes, and when your personal impressions of the subject are clear and strong, you need to ask yourself what should be of interest to your reader. What will cause him to identify with the subject? What will arouse his interest? The news reporter, as you know, relies on the what, when, where and who of his story to satisfy the curiosity of his reader. The writer of other than news stories will find it expedient to emphasize the how and the why also. You may recall that in the Preface I related that the editor of the *Times* Sunday travel section wanted me to "tell the people what a cottonmouth is and how to get there, what the accommodations are and so on." In my ignorance at the time, I had failed to tell it all, and if the piece had run without full information, readers would have let the editor know of their frustration. Putting yourself in the reader's place, ask yourself if what you have written leaves any important question unanswered.

In this connection, you have doubtless been interested at one time or another in visiting a museum or other attraction that you have read about, only to find that there was a missing ingredient which cooled off your interest. Perhaps the piece failed to say whether or not the place was open on Sunday. Perhaps you actually arrived at the door only to find that a reservation was needed, although the article had not mentioned it.

To distill a rule out of this, let us say—give all the information and give it accurately.

Before putting word to paper, it is smart also to consider what the story line or theme should be in terms of the kind of material you have. If you're writing a "stray dog" story, you would do the obvious—engage the reader's sympathy with the dog. You would hardly write a diatribe against the poor, innocent, neglected animal. The story line, in essence, is a thread of particular interest that runs throughout the story. More descriptively, perhaps, it is the main artery, which has various little side branches of interest that diverge for a moment and return, contributing their flavor to the main course, or flow. A story theme is present in any set of facts that you have accumulated and wish to use in writing an article. It is a matter of recognizing it, choosing it and following it. To follow the central theme makes for unity in the piece, keeps the story on the track and leads inevitably to a conclusion. The story doesn't wobble feebly to a close—it strides there deliberately.

From the point of view of the reader, who is your ultimate critic, a story that hangs together is worth his attention; one that wanders or drifts aimlessly is a waste of his time.

To write the story well demands recognition of a set of "eternal verities" which playwrights know about. These verities for writers dictate that there must be for every story a beginning, a middle and an end, of which the most difficult, as you are likely to discover for yourself, are the beginning and the end. The geographical middle seems to fit in between without too much trouble.

To begin with the beginning—the best of the world's writers have had trouble getting started on a piece of writing. We can sum up the situation for all of them here by quoting an excerpt from Hemingway's *The Moveable Feast*, published by Charles Scribner's Sons.

". . . Sometimes when I was starting a new story and I could not get it going . . . I would write one true sentence, and then go on from there. . . . If I started to write elaborately, or like someone introducing or presenting something, I found that I could cut that scrollwork or ornament out and throw it away and start with the first true simple declarative sentence I had written."

In another area of writing—that of the advertising copy-writer—in which space restrictions do not permit slow starts and no words are to be wasted, an axiom was current at one time which advised the writer to "begin with the second paragraph." This was recognition that writers in that field, particularly less experienced ones, were often prone to take or need time to warm up to the subject. If you, yourself, were to look right now at some of the pieces that you wrote some time ago, the likelihood is that you would agree with the "second paragraph" approach.

Having found a good beginning sentence and paragraph that will "grab" the reader's attention and whet his appetite for more, the writer can settle down to the meat of his story—the bulk of the piece, the middle part. Here, he draws the big picture, leading the reader through the scene, sketching in a detail here and adding a fact there, moving his explanations deftly from area to area until the reader becomes fully aware of the story as a whole. In this middle part, the writer can afford to—in fact, must—give rein to his skills in order to avoid the creeping kind of dullness that tends to set in when an account is written from the purely sequential and factual point-of-view. After getting the story moving, he must keep it going, playing the tone up or down on occasion by dropping in tidbits of information about the subject that have unusual elements of interest. He shouldn't use up all his good stuff at one place in the story. Before the reader knows it, he will be anticipating these touches of flavor and his interest and expectation will remain high.

The middle area is also where the writer can play around successfully with the side effects that branch out from the central theme. Whether he brings them in directly or subtly will depend upon his own flow of thought as he writes, but in either case they are enormously important to reader interest, and a writer who knows how to weave them into the pattern has a built-in lure that hooks the reader every time. This process can be likened to the occasional pat given to the rolling hoop to keep up its momentum.

The end of the story comes when there is nothing left to be said. You have "said your piece," as the phrase goes, but it is not enough to stop dead. You are not likely to know at the beginning what your final sentence or paragraph is going to be. Good writing is, for me at least, not cold-bloodedly contrived or formularized. But, as you see the end approaching, you also see a natural way of putting the final period to it. Your conclusion is a rounding out of the story, which to my mind is never a straight-line affair, but always a circle. You can complete this circle in several ways, according to the needs of the particular story. If you've written a travel article with such blandishment that your reader can't wait to get started, the best thing to close with is what he wants most to know—tell him how to get there. Of course, you wouldn't have thrown in such side-tracking details before building up interest in the subject. You need not moralize, point-up or urge action.

If, on the other hand, your article is about a personality, a natural kind of conclusion might be concerned with an observation about that personality drawn from the facts of his character or skills. If it is about an event that evokes some kind of feeling, such as nostalgia, or sets a mood or atmosphere, a conclusion can often be beautifully derived from the use of an allusion or an appropriate quotation.

Regardless of the method used in concluding your article or story, it must be kept in mind that the purpose is to tie up the package for the reader, none of whom likes or appreciates being left dangling.

Among my own pieces, I have come across a short one (1,000 words) that will serve here to delineate construction, with particular reference to the beginning, middle and end. It appeared in *The New York Times* in August, 1966.

Meylin's gunshop.

FEUD OVER A STRAIGHT-SHOOTIN' RIFLE

Lancaster, Pa.—A mild controversy erupts regularly in these parts over whether the gun that "won the war for independence," defeated the British at New Orleans and opened the West to settlement should rightfully be called the Pennsylvania rifle or the Kentucky rifle. Partisans of both states who still possess the rifles shoot it out every few years in friendly competition. Judging from the

The Lancaster County Historical Society agrees with the Commonwealth in this sign on Meylin's gunshop.

score so far, it appears that the rifle deserves to be named for Kentucky.

On the other hand, Pennsylvanians defend their stand by pointing to a stone cabin near Lancaster in which Martin Meylin is said to have invented the rifle in the early 1700s. The Commonwealth of Pennsylvania has supported this claim by planting bronze markers in concrete on U.S. 30, at the approaches to the city. The markers state categorically that the Kentucky rifle had its origin here, and, in effect, is travelling through history under an assumed name.

The truth seems to be that the Pennsylvania rifle lost its identity after the Revolutionary War when, in the hands of such notable travelers as Daniel Boone and Davy Crockett and the host of frontiersmen who had served in the army, it was carried westward into Ohio and Kentucky. When many of the men later floated down the Mississippi on barges to fight the Battle of New Orleans, they sang the roisterous song, "Hunters of Kentucky," and the name stuck to the rifle they carried.

On September 5, travelers will have a chance to see the Kentucky rifle in action. An informal shoot will be held at The Eagle, a gun museum run by Vincent W. Nolt on State Route 741 in nearby Strasburg. Mr. Nolt owns one of the largest collections of Kentuckys, each rifle different and each a fine example of the personalized, muzzle-loading flintlocks that helped open the American wilderness.

The shoot will be held in a field adjacent to The Eagle, which is a reconstructed grist and whisky mill on Pequea Creek. The visitor will be permitted to take a shot himself, if he wishes. In so doing, he may sense how a Colonial hunter, a farmer or a backwoodsman felt as he drew a bead on a squirrel high in a tree, or on an Indian or a running deer.

The experience should help the visitor to understand why British soldiers came to fear this long, straight-shooting rifle and why, according to a historian, Joseph Kindig, Jr., an American captive was taken to England to demonstrate its qualities.

A close look at one of the Kentuckys should lead to an appreciation of the workmanship of the early Lancaster County gunsmiths, particularly as shown in the embellishments along the barrel and on the stock and patchbox. Decorative carvings on the curly maple stock, engraved patchbox covers of brass and inlaid silver ornaments make each gun a work of art and express something of what each owner felt for his rifle. It was never out of his sight, never far from hand.

Riflemen at the shoot will be decked out in frontier style: coonskin hats, fringed buckskins and moccasins, powder horn hung from the shoulder and a leather pouch for lead shot, and a Bowie knife at the belt. And the distinctive crack of the long rifle that echoed through the woods and across the valleys of 18th century America will be heard again.

The route to The Eagle from Lancaster passes within half a mile of Martin Meylin's gunshop. The little stone building is now abandoned, but it is still in fair shape. In it, Meylin, a Swiss gunsmith, is said to have conceived the idea of combining the best features of the short German rifle with those of the English long-barreled, smooth-bore fowling piece.

The result was a long rifle capable of shooting far and straight,

Vincent W. Nolt, proprietor of the Eagle, dressed for action and armed to the teeth with rifle, bowie knife and tomahawk. A good rifle is worth several thousand dollars and the trading is brisk. (Photo courtesy of Mr. Nolt)

and powerful enough to kill game or foe at previously unheard-of distances. It is documented that, at the siege of Boston, "a rifleman, who, upon seeing some British on a scow at a distance of fully half a mile, found a good resting place on a hill and bombarded them until he potted the lot."

To get to the shop from Lancaster, take U.S. 222 south about

While doing the Kentucky Rifle story for the *Times*, I set up a rifle and powder horn against an old millstone that was leaning against the Eagle Museum in order to get a shot of some of the gun's details. Note the bird's nest to the right of the center hole in the stone.

four miles to its junction with State Route 72. Turn left on U.S. 222 and left again almost immediately on the first road, which is Eshleman Mill Road. Meylin's gunshop is about half a mile farther, at the left of the road.

To reach The Eagle, return to U.S. 222 and turn left. In about a mile, turn left on State Route 741. The Eagle is a few minutes away. Total distance from Lancaster is eight or nine miles.

The Eagle, which serves as a museum for Americana as well as for guns, is open from 10 A.M. to 5 P.M. on weekdays and from noon to 7 P.M. on weekends. It is closed for the season at the end of October.

You will note that the three opening paragraphs set the scene for the story as a whole, in which the Kentucky rifle plays the dominant part. The next several paragraphs begin the middle section by bringing in the contest at The Eagle, thus involving the reader with the possibility of seeing the rifle in action in person and even of trying a shot himself. The following paragraphs, still in the middle, go into more detail about the rifle and the shoot. They sustain interest through the use of little tributary bits of information about the rifle. The final three paragraphs round out the piece with directions and other useful information for the reader who, having learned about the shoot and The Eagle, wants to go there to see the rifle in action.

I mentioned in an earlier chapter that one way to find a story is to recognize it in a news item and then to investigate the possibility. This is how I learned about The Eagle and the up-coming shoot there. The photographer alone or the writer alone could have followed this lead and have come up with something to sell. From the photographic angle, good pictures abound—Meylin's gunshop, the rifle, the shoot, the costumes, The Eagle inside and outside. From the writer's viewpoint, the material is so abundant that his main job is deciding what not to include, but since he can pick and choose, he can select for the story (keep in mind that for the purpose it could not be longer) information that best aroused and retained reader interest. Obviously, this story is perfect for the person—the writer-photographer—who can use both the camera and the typewriter. For the photographer, the story demonstrates, I think, how words can be used to go with pictures; and for the writer there can be little doubt about the value and desirability of getting and using pictures.

The foregoing story makes use of narration and description to carry its message. The somewhat longer piece which follows also tells a story and describes a scene, but adds argumentation which, in this case, results in a kind of plea for action. It is of interest here to compare the two in order to show something of a range for the skills of the writer-photographer. The story is No. 20 of *The Printed Page*, a publication of The Maple Press of York, Pennsylvania, and is called:

THE MILL OF LINCHESTER

One would be hard put to it to put his finger quickly on the kind of private business enterprise that has operated longest in this country. In what area would it lie—transportation, printing, automobiles, shipping, mining, communications, farming, food processing? Some other, perhaps?

The answer is milling—flour milling. That is the category, but what about the one—single—privately undertaken and privately run business in that category that has lasted longer than any other? What and where is the oldest established business in the United States that is still functioning?

It is a one-man grist mill on Maryland's Eastern Shore, and it has never stopped grinding corn since the year it was built . . . 1681. You can walk through its doorway today and buy a bag of corn meal that is exactly the same kind as was bought there by a settler of more than 280 years ago. The mill has always been open for business, except for occasional shutdowns for repairs.

It is difficult, if not impossible, to grasp the significance of the working life of this mill simply by knowing the year of its founding. What are 200 years in point of time or history compared with . . . "the glory that was Greece, and the grandeur that was Rome"? But in this country, a couple of centuries take us back to before our existence as a world state. A lot of water has flowed over the mill dam since the United States set up its own shop, and a lot more turned the mill wheel in the 95 years of its life before the American Revolution.

Perhaps it will help in the conception of time, American style, to say that the Maryland mill began its long business life only 72 years after Henry Hudson set up a trading post in a place called New York, and only 61 years after some people who called themselves Pilgrims stepped ashore in Massachusetts.

Perhaps it will help even more to point out that the mill was grinding corn before William Penn founded Philadelpha; before Bunker Hill; before the discovery of the North Pole and the South Pole; before the invention of radio, the airplane, the steamship, the electric light, the telephone, the automobile, the railroad; before, in fact, practically anything and everything that affect our lives today.

And today, when we have in this country transportation faster than sound, and nuclear power, and automation, and the computer, and the technology to send men to the moon, we still have in daily operation the ancient mill that grinds corn just as it used to do before the occurrence of all these world-shaking events. The mill and its owner are a sort of Eighth Wonder of the World . . . American Free Enterprise in Action.

* * *

On Hunting Creek, which flows from Linchester Pond, in Caroline County, Maryland, a man named Frank S. Langrell operates Linchester Mill today. Maryland State Route 331 runs between the pond and the mill, and a state marker about ten miles southeast of Easton identifies the place. Mr. Langrell, known locally as Captain, typifies in himself something that has kept the old mill going—the power of endurance. He has owned and operated the mill single-handedly for more than fifty years, and worked there as a helper for fifteen years before that. At 83 years of age, the Captain personifies the rugged individualism of the independent man who makes his way through life by hard work and with a persistent spirit that keeps him, as they used to say, "beholden to none."

Something of the miller's character and attitudes is exemplified by anecdotes about him that appeared a couple of years ago in a *New York Times* story.

"No captain was ever more independent. Once . . . he repelled what he considered an invasion of his rights by the Office of Price Administration. When a representative kept insisting on detailed reports of the mill's production, the captain drove him off the premises by hurling a scoopful of flour into his face." Captain Langrell simply couldn't and wouldn't countenance interference in

A photograph of a roadside historical marker such as this is often published as an inset of another photograph to save space. The words serve as a caption or legend for the main photo.

his business by the United States Government or by anybody else. His forthright, determined and direct action worked wonders . . . he was never bothered again.

"Not too long ago," said the *Times*, "Captain Langrell was assaulted in an attempted hold-up by a man posing as a seller of

The Miller of Linchester—a study of a man of independent character. I asked him to stand by the door—then let the light play upon his features and the lines of his clothing. The effect, I think, carries something of pathos. The picture was used in *The Printed Page*.

corn. In the struggle, a hard blow on the miller's old head caused a
gash requiring 15 stitches. Although quite stunned, the miller did
not go down." He was 81 years old at the time. When asked how
he had managed to keep his feet, he replied, "I've been standing up
so long, I guess I didn't know how to fall."

A man who doesn't know how to fall, nor to bow in submission
before a bureaucrat is in the mold of other heroes whose deeds dot
the pages of history . . . Leonidas at Thermopylae, Andy Jackson
at New Orleans, Washington at Valley Forge.

This man and his mill seem to belie their individual strength: the
man, a fragile-looking lightweight; the mill, a nondescript wood
structure. But the spirit of the one and the oaken bones of the other
prove their virtue.

Linchester Mill, which once catered to the needs of colonists
and settlers, Indians and farmers, and even sent corn meal to
Washington's men at Valley Forge, now grinds the same meal for
small stores and people who live in surrounding Caroline and
Dorchester Counties. Two hundred years ago, a man on foot or on
horseback stopped at the mill's Dutch door for a pouchful of meal;
today, he comes in a high-powered automobile and picks up a two-
pound package of the Captain's product, neatly labelled "Linchester
Roller Mills—Fresh Water-Ground Corn Meal—Manufactured by
Frank S. Langrell." In earlier times, the Captain delivered his
packaged meal by horse and buggy; today he makes his deliveries
in a pickup truck every Thursday, the only day of the week except
Sunday that the mill is closed.

On any other day, the visitor to Linchester Mill can see Free
Enterprise at work . . . a man doing what he knows best and
doing it according to his own standards and in the realization that
his responsibility is to himself alone. On this basis, the miller of
Linchester has kept the mill going and made an honest living for
nearly seventy years. His predecessors at the mill in the long line of
years before the Captain took the helm passed into the background
of the mill's history quietly, each man surrendering in the end to
anonymity. Their deeds, such as they might have been, are un-
recorded. The one thread that bound them all together for close to
three centuries, and that tells us something of their character, is the
mill itself. They all spent their days in its dusty rooms, grinding

corn and wheat, talking to their customers when they were on hand to pass on the news, grinding, as it were, their daily bread, and—above all—"earning their keep." Throughout the long stretch of their tenure, the millstone rumbled and wore out and rumbled and wore out again—and again; the overshot water wheel turned and clanked, and started and stopped in response to the touch of the miller's hand on the sluice gate control; and overall, in summer and winter, and every day since 1681, was the sound of water—in full splash when the grinding was good, and in tinklings and drippings when things were slow, and at night time. Thus, Linchester Mill survived all of its millers, each in turn both its master and its slave. But all kept it going and spent their lives in its service, in return for which the mill performed its ancient and elemental function of grinding grain to feed the people within its reaches.

The people of the 17th century who depended upon Linchester Mill, and those of the 18th and 19th centuries, would doubtless have marveled at the tough quality of *their* mill which made it last so long in service beyond their own times. To them, the mill was a deep necessity. To those few who buy and enjoy its products today, the mill is a link with the past when life was more simple and its pleasures less frenetic. To others who drive swiftly by Linchester Pond, the sturdy, old building at the end of the mill race is just that and nothing more. To them, the question would be, if any arose at all . . . "Of what importance is an old grist mill when men fly to the moon?"

* * *

America's greatness as a nation lies on the fundamental opportunity given every man to find his way through life on his own merit. To succeed, one works and earns what he deserves in proportion to the need for his goods and services. Sometimes a grateful or appreciative government or industry recognizes its founders and heroes by building beautiful memorials to them—the carving of mountains, setting up museums, setting aside and displaying prototypes, even restoring and preserving significant parts of their heritage. Sometimes, too, the obvious is overlooked.

Down along the Maryland shore, Linchester Mill appears in the minds of many to be worthy of preservation as a pre-colonial business enterprise, as the Hopewell Village iron foundry is in

Pennsylvania. Is iron more basic than grain? Has any other private business anywhere in the country functioned longer than Linchester Mill? The answer, of course, is negative.

You will have observed that the construction of the Linchester Mill story includes two elements that are not present, nor needed, in the Kentucky Rifle story. The first is a preamble which sets the stage for the account of the mill and the miller, and since it is a distinctly separate entity is set apart by asterisks. The same is true of the peroration—the second element—a sort of rhetorical summing up. Both elements were necessary to the purpose of the piece, which was to describe the mill and its history (the middle part) and to stir up some interest in preserving the mill as an historic site. With only slight modifications, the longer part between the asterisks could stand on its own as a story similar in character to that of the Kentucky Rifle article. In fact, Linchester Mill did run in the *Times* in a shorter and totally different version which I handled as an assignment from the editor.

Because I am such a firm believer in the effectiveness of opening a story or article with a paragraph that catches the reader's attention, I think it expedient here to mention a device I have used where circumstances permitted. Unlike the pre-amble of the Linchester story and the more usual opening of the Kentucky rifle article, this device makes use of the shock value of strong contrast. It forces the reader's imagination to come into play and makes it difficult for him not to read on. It makes him want to know what happens next. Such an opening paragraph follows, quoted from an issue of *The Printed Page* called *Voyage of the Codorus:*

The British liner, *Queen Elizabeth,* displaces 83,673 tons, is 1,031 feet long and 118 feet, 7 inches wide. With her 200,000 h.p. at

"How amazing that a farmer should be splitting wood to produce energy (to heat his home) while his next-door neighbors at the atomic plant were splitting atoms for the same purpose!"

work, she can move along at close to 40 miles an hour, and cross an ocean in a few days and hours. The American steamboat, *Codorus,* on the other hand and at the other end of the statistical scale, weighed only 6 tons, was only 60 feet long and 9 feet wide. Her engine developed 10 h.p. and in calm water she could speed along at about 7 miles an hour. Despite the wide differences in the personal statistics of the two vessels, a basis exists for comparing them —for putting them, as it were, "in the same boat." Both fit into the category of "iron steamship." And there all similarity ends between a great ocean liner of today and a riverboat of almost 150 years ago. Small as she was, however, the *Codorus* earned as many distinctions as did her big sister. She was the first iron steamboat to navigate an American inland waterway, the first and only steamboat to ascend the Susquehanna River into New York State, and the first vessel to use anthracite coal as fuel. Her trip up-river (in 1826) was a breathless, 300-mile, 3-month adventure. (The remainder of the story describes the adventure.)

Still another device that is helpful in writing the story and that should be brought in early is best described as a peg to hang the story on. It is a thought or observation which is striking enough in character to catch the reader's imagination. It has within it the elements of intrigue and noteworthiness, and a kind of nagging quality that persists and remains unforgettable. The effectiveness of such a peg depends upon its unvarnished naturalness, its obvious suitability. If at all contrived or forced or striven for, its weakness becomes evident and its effectiveness is lost. Such a peg usually reveals itself in a flash and as a matter of course when the writer is considering his story.

As an example, I cite the instance when, as I was tracking down the story about the Peach Bottom atomic power plant, I stopped the car a mile away from the plant to admire a rural scene—Holstein cows grazing in a pasture that sloped upward toward farm buildings and a country church. I could hear the

"Atom splitter on the sleepy Susquehanna."

blow of an axe as the unseen farmer split wood. The thought struck me instantly; how amazing that a farmer should be splitting wood to produce energy (to heat his home) while his next-door neighbors at the atomic plant were splitting atoms for the same purpose! The ancient way and the modern in such close juxtaposition became the peg for the story.

Although the devices and methods mentioned have their value and are important in writing a story, they do not overshadow the writer's basic arsenal of words. They are the tools of his trade and, as it is with every workman, the better he knows his tools the better the job he can do. A solid vocabulary is, therefore, a necessity. Plainly, the more words he knows and the more he knows of their origins the better able he is to understand their meanings and to transmit his thought exactly to the minds of his readers. He will be able to select the best word to carry his meaning; his readers will be able to understand precisely what he is saying. In such a writer-reader relationship, nothing is lost in translation because nothing intrudes to disrupt the sweet flow of thought—no word that is almost right is there to raise the eyebrow of the knowing reader, no word that screams of its mis-use is there to insult the reader's intelligence, no "sore-thumb" word is there to distract the reader's attention. This ideal flow of meaning suggests a fitting line from Shakespeare—" 'tis a consummation devoutly to be wish'd." It is, however, a consummation arrived at not often enough.

The writer, then, must know words. He must also know the ground-rules of his language so that he can string his words together logically and effectively. If he uses simple declarative sentences only, he will drive his reader away (not to say his editor) in three seconds flat. Accordingly, he will vary his sentence structure to include the many forms available, and so avoid dreary dullness and maintain interest. He will recognize that good writing relies upon the use of strong, vigorous verbs and distinctive nouns, and that all other words are in one way or another qualifiers or connectives . . . not the real guts of the sentence. Whenever he can, he will lean toward words rooted in the Anglo-Saxon, rather than those that come from Latin and Greek. They're quicker, more vigorous, less cumbersome.

With something to say and words to say it with, writing the story becomes a physical thing—you have to write the words on paper. This is not as easy as it sounds. Remember Hemingway's trouble in getting started. There's something about that blank page in your typewriter that challenges you to put something down that makes sense. As you face the page and arrange yourself comfortably, a hundred paragraph openings flow through your mind, offering themselves one after the other and each saying, Try me! The best thing to do is to plunge in. Take any one of them. Put it down. You can always throw it out later if you like. Once you've started, you have hurdled the opening barrier and the field opens before you.

Keep in mind that you are not writing a finished draft. You are simply roughing out the canvas, laying the groundwork for the finer, final touches. Accordingly, you can go as fast as your thoughts and your typing skill will let you, and you can x-out one bad word and write in another as often as you please without worrying about what the page looks like. In this fashion, you can wrestle your way through to the end of the article. At this point, my advice is to let your writing gel overnight. Put it aside and forget it until tomorrow.

So far you have been totally subjective, but when you look at your writing again you see it in a different light—you see it more objectively, perhaps as the reader sees it. It appears almost as though someone else had written it. You spot errors of one sort or another. You may even wonder how you could have said what you did. You notice that you have used the same word too many times. As you read the piece through, a new or better thought might occur. You correct and change, and

depending upon how messed up the first draft is, you retype
it so that you can read it through smoothly without having to
disrupt its flow because of the need to interpret your markings.
If your editing of the first draft has left it fairly clean, you
might be able to go directly to the final draft on white paper.

Here, a surprising thing often happens. Although you have
read and corrected and revised your first draft, and have re-read
it several times, you are likely to find yourself making occasional changes as you write the final draft. You are not hunting
for changes to make—the new thought simply pops up, inspired
by some process of the mind at that instant. Such changes, I
have found, are generally good ones, fitting naturally into the
paragraph.

With the final sheet out of the typewriter, one important
thing remains to be done. Check the piece from end to end
for typographical errors, misspelled words and general accuracy.

In rounding out the matter of writing the story, a word
should be said about the length of the piece—the number of
words to write. This has plagued many a beginning writer, the
more experienced having learned by doing. It should be obvious, I think, that the writer should never use more words
than he needs to tell his story, which is based on the material
he has to work with. A solid article can be written on a given
subject—and so can a book. It all depends on the end in view
(the market you are aiming at) and the depth to which you
wish to go in treating the subject. There is more on the market
in a later chapter, but for the moment, since we are dealing
with the writing itself, it is pertinent to warn against the effort
to pad an article in order to meet an editorial requirement. Let
us say, for instance, that the paper or magazine to which you
intend to submit your story requires 1,000 to 1,500 words.
You would naturally structure your story to fall within these
limits, for if you wrote below or above them to any degree
you would have failed to recognize the restriction and rejec-

tion would follow. To attempt to pad the material to meet the minimum requirement would have the same result. Editors are not stupid. They can spot what does not belong. Any good writer, however, writes on the basis of his own integrity and avoids the possibility of building a poor reputation.

6

Photography For The Writer–The Camera And Its Uses

A camera is a box having a small hole at one side to admit light, a piece of film at the opposite side which receives the light, and a means of admitting and shutting off the light. A comparably simple definition of a story would be that it consists of one or more sheets of paper on which words are written. Although the elemental truth exists in both definitions, we would hardly undertake, in either case, to follow the definition in the belief that we would produce anything worthwhile.

One or another of the big-name professional photographers has been known to fool around with a homemade cardboard camera from time to time, and to get a picture from it, but he does it for fun. When he is at work, you can be sure that he depends on the most sophisticated photographic equipment available, most of it extremely complicated in construction and function. The simplest automatic camera in use today is a complex machine; the camera that permits individual control of various functions is far more so. My own camera, for instance, is not unusual for its kind in having more than 900 parts. The simple pressing of the button sets in motion numerous mechanical and electronic functions every time an exposure is made. Fortunately, it is unnecessary to be a scientist or an engineer to press the button. What is necessary is an understanding of a few principles which apply no matter what kind of camera you use. With them in mind and thorough knowledge of the capabilities of your camera, you can take publishable pictures to go with your articles regardless of the working conditions you run into.

At the bottom of it, all cameras are the same in that they have a lens through which light passes, a diaphragm which controls the amount of light, a shutter which controls the time of exposure, and, of course, a ring which moves the lens toward or away from the film plane to bring the subject into proper focus. To take a good picture, then, is a matter of selecting the shutter speed and diaphragm opening which permit the correct amount of light to reach the film under any given condition, and to focus so that the image of the subject is sharp and clear.

The differences among kinds of cameras are mainly in size, lenses, methods of operation, versatility and capability. For the purposes of the writer-photographer, there is no point in discussing types other than those that can be of practical use to him. Of these, two are worthy of serious consideration as your No. 1 camera—the twin lens reflex and the single lens reflex. When you use either or both of them, you are in good company, for the world's best photojournalists prefer them as standard equipment. The kinds of cameras seen most frequently, however, are the little automatics that take drop-in film cartridges, and the "instant replay" Polaroid that delivers the picture in a minute or so. Wherever the tourists are and wherever you see groups of any kind on excursion or strolling in the park on a Sunday afternoon, there you will see these popular cameras. As was the case with the old Brownie box camera, they satisfy the needs of the snapshooter. But for the writer-photographer or the photojournalist they lack versatility and adaptability, and are simply not up to the job that has to be done.

The twin lens reflex has a viewing lens and a taking lens. The photographer looks down into the top of the camera where he sees the image of his subject. By using a knob which moves the lens backward or forward, he brings the image into focus. Because this kind of camera uses a relatively large film, each frame or picture seen in the viewer gives the photographer the opportunity to focus and compose in close detail, and what he sees when he shoots is what he will get in the finished print. Light from the subject enters the camera through one of the lenses and produces the image seen through the viewer. Light also reaches the film through the other lens and when the shutter is released records the image on the film.

The single lens reflex, now commonly referred to as SLR, admits light to the eye and to the film through one lens only. The photographer views his subject by holding the camera to his eye. Light is reflected by a mirror and a prism within the camera body, so that the subject is clearly seen through the eye level viewer. The subject is brought into focus by turning the lens in or out, and is composed within the frame at the moment of shooting. When the shutter is released the mirror flips up out of the way of the light entering the lens, thus permitting the light to reach the film.

These are the basic differences in operation between the two reflex cameras. Each kind of camera has advantages and disadvantages, with the SLR today having, in my opinion, more advantages and fewer disadvantages. In this respect, I am not alone, for almost all professionals now use the SLR. Still, it was only a few years back when staff photographers made their reputations, while working for such publications as *Life* and *Look*, using twin lens reflexes. As the SLR system was developed, the same photographers swung over to the SLR, having recognized their superiority in one area or another, but not necessarily in quality of picture. The likelihood is that many if not all of these photographers use the SLR most of the time and the twin lens on occasion. But, for the purposes of the writer-photographer the SLR is sufficient unto itself and there is no need to have both.

As I see it and from my own experience with both kinds of camera, the twin lens has two basic faults, both serious. One is that it is necessary to look down into the viewer instead of viewing the scene at eye level as with the SLR. This is an inconvenience, if that is a strong enough word, which often prevents the taking of a picture. Here's a case in point. I was sitting in my parked car along a roadside in the Amish country of Pennsylvania. My twin lens Yashica was on the seat beside me. Suddenly, a horse and buggy came dashing around the bend a short distance ahead, driven by a young Amishman dressed in black from head to foot except for the brilliant blue of his shirt. His beard was red and his bright teeth flashed in a broad grin as he came on driving hard. He was enjoying his moment of freedom away from the usual sombre quality of his life on the farm—he was a sportsman testing out his Alfa-Romeo. I had about ten seconds to do something. I grabbed the camera and cranked up the shutter. Hoping to get a head-on shot through the windshield, I looked down into the viewfinder and could see nothing except the dashboard of the car. With an eye level SLR, I could have had the picture. Of course, I could have held the camera high enough and, without viewing the scene at all, taken a chance shot. But there was no time.

The same sort of awkwardness in viewing with the twin lens comes into play when you want to photograph something that is directly below you, as for instance a pebble on the beach from a standing position, or a close-up of a document that is on a flat or horizontal plane such as a table top. By looking down, as you have to with a twins lens, you would not be able to see the image in the viewfinder at all. To get such a picture you have to hold the camera outstretched with the viewing area facing you—a clumsy thing at best.

A more serious fault is concerned with the design and construction of the twin lens camera which does not take into account the need for interchangeability of lenses. Up until now, the twin lens system used fixed lenses, and the capability of the camera depended upon the lens that came with it. The photographer could not switch to a long lens (telephoto) or to a wide-angle when the shot to be made required it. As a consequence, the camera was severely limited. However, this fault is being corrected in newly designed twin lens cameras which will have the capability of using different lenses.

A minor fault with the twin lens, but still a fault, is concerned with the size of the film it uses. Because it is larger than that of the SLR, there are fewer frames or picture areas to the roll, and as a consequence you have to change film more often. It is surprising how quickly you use up a roll.

About the only advantage of the twin lens camera that I know of is, again, concerned with the film. Since it produces bigger negatives, it has greater capability for enlargement without undue graininess, particularly with the faster films which, when enlarged, are prone to show grain. However, even this advantage is somewhat dubious because for the purpose of the writer-photographer, which is production of high quality 8 by 10 or 5 by 7 photographs suitable for reproduction in newspapers and magazines, the smaller-negative SLR camera does offer enlargement to those sizes without obvious graininess. The advantage of the twin lens film size applies, therefore, only when the photographer is concerned with oversize enlargements such as salon prints or murals.

Plainly, in a comparison of this sort, the disadvantage of one camera is the advantage of the other; but it might be well to sum up and emphasize the reasons why the SLR is the preferred camera for the writer-photographer. It offers eye level viewing which is quick and convenient. It permits the photographer to change from one lens to another in order to meet given situations and, in fact, to get pictures under conditions that would not yield pictures with fixed lens cameras. Its film cartridge holds 20 or 36 frames as opposed to a dozen or so, thus enabling the photographer to work longer before changing film. It provides many other extras for a kind of versatility unequalled by

One reason why you need a fast lens—to get the rare mood shot when no other lens will do the job. Here, the author's wife is caught by a 50mm, f/1.4 lens in low light conditions.

the twin lens or other kinds of cameras. My SLR, for instance, lets me see the depth-of-field through the lens when I depress a preview button; it accepts different viewing screens for specific purposes; it has a handy timing device and a built-in light meter exposure system. The SLR, in short, is made to order for the writer-photographer.

It has been said by many a writer on photography that no single lens is best for all picture taking situations. Thus, the feature that makes the SLR ideal is its ability to use various lenses depending on need. Its second most important feature, to me, is its eye level viewfinder. With only these two virtues, the SLR design can turn any reasonably intelligent snapshooting writer into a respectable taker of pictures that will complement the quality of his writing. Keeping in mind that picture quality must be considerably better than mediocre and that the SLR is a machine that is only as good as the man who is using it, it will behoove the aforesaid intelligent writer to learn what his particular camera is capable of doing and to understand the characteristics of lenses—normal, wide-angle and long (or telephoto). Whatever else that can be picked up through practice and experience can be put to use as learned, but without a thorough understanding of your own photographic equipment at the very beginning, you may never be able to put it to full use and may perpetuate your errors. The idea, of course, is to become as familiar with your camera as you are with your typewriter. The time will come sooner than you expect when you can put aside your instruction manual altogether.

Earlier in this chapter, the basics of camera operation were touched upon lightly. Without knowing what kind of camera you will settle on, it is impossible here to discuss its details. It will be up to you and your instruction manual. On the other hand, it is possible, assuming that you will choose an SLR, to go into the fundamentals of lenses and what they can do for your picture taking.

Lenses fall into three groups insofar as the general, as opposed to the specialized, photographer is concerned. We might call them short, medium and long. They are all categorized by their focal lengths in millimeters. Thus, in the short or wide-angle group are the 15mm, 21mm, 25mm, 28mm and 35mm lenses; in the medium or normal group are the 50mm, 55mm and 58mm lenses; and in the long or telephoto group are lenses ranging from 85mm to 1200mm. For our purposes we can eliminate consideration of the extremes in these groups—the 21mm and 25mm wide angles and the long lenses above 135mm —because these are really special lenses for unusual purposes and are not likely to find use in the hands of the writer-photographer. We can concentrate on the characteristics and qualities of those that remain and make a selection from them.

It is necessary first to define and understand a few terms relating to lenses. Each lens is marked according to its focal length—28mm, 135mm and so on—which in essence is the distance from the lens to the film. This is a simplified definition, a more exact one being the distance from the central area of the lens to the focal plane, but it is sufficient to get the idea across. In effect then, the farther away that a lens is from the film, the longer the focal length of the lens. It is important to understand this because of the implications of focal length with respect to two notable characteristics of lenses—the angle-of-view and depth-of-field. If you know what a given lens can do, you will be able to choose the right lens to handle the photographic problem that faces you.

The normal or standard lens (50mm, 55mm or 58mm) is so called because its viewing angle, or what you see through the viewfinder and get in the picture, approximates what your eye sees when looking straight ahead. This is the lens that the manufacturer usually includes with the camera when you buy it. With a viewing angle of 46 degrees, the 50mm lens has less capacity to broaden the picture than the wide-angle lenses with viewing angles of approximately 60 to 180 degrees, and more capacity than the long lenses which have viewing angles that become smaller as the focal length increases. To say it another way, the shorter the focal length of a lens, the wider the view; and the longer the focal length, the narrower and more concentrated the view.

The second characteristic of lenses is depth-of-field. Theoretically, there is only one plane in a picture that is in focus, but for all practical purposes that plane becomes an area or zone of sharpness in front of and behind the subject being photographed. This area of acceptable sharpness varies with, and is an inherent capability or characteristic of, a given lens. In general, depth-of-field is greatest with the wide-angle lenses and becomes progressively less with the longer focal lengths of the normal through the telephoto lenses.

We can sum up these two characteristics of lenses—angle-of-view and depth-of-field—in a single easy-to-remember statement: the shorter the lens (wide-angles), the wider the view and the greater the depth-of-field; and the longer the lens (telephotos), the narrower the view and the depth-of-field.

It might logically be asked at this point why a long lens is necessary at all since the wide-angle lens covers a wider area and has a greater depth-of-field. Why not a single lens to do everything? A good question—but one that is easily satisfied. It is technically and for practical purposes impossible for one lens to do everything you want it to do. For instance, if you want to single out a face in a crowd, in which case you wouldn't care a jot or a tittle about depth-of-field or wide viewing angle, you would have to use a long lens—the only lens that would do the job; or if you want to get the architectural detail of the gable end of a three-story house where depth-of-field is unimportant, you would choose your long lens. Also, with the long lens you can make its lack of depth-of-field work to your advantage, as, for instance, in taking a portrait of a head and shoulders from five feet away. In this case, you do not want hard sharpness which would show every facial blemish, and you do not want distracting background. Your long lens would give you a soft-focus portrait that fills the picture and minimizes or obliterates background.

Since the long lens narrows the scene and concentrates the picture, it is possible to utilize the film frame to its fullest, giving you large prints with little or no wasted frame area. Keep in mind that the long lens brings the subject closer. You must keep in mind also that since the long lens has little depth-of-field when the subject is fairly close to the camera it is necessary to focus as closely as possible. This is not necessary if the subject, for instance a mountain goat in its natural habitat, is far away and nothing intervenes between the camera and the subject. You would simply set the lens at infinity and fire away, knowing that the long lens would bring the subject closer and that it would be in focus. In a word, with long lenses narrow depth-of-field makes focusing critical when the subject is close to the camera, and it matters less when the subject is hundreds or thousands of feet away.

The wide-angle lens is necessary because its wide viewing ability and great depth-of-field make it possible to take pictures in situations where neither the normal lens nor the telephoto would be effective. When the subject is close to you and you can't back up any more, only the wide-angle lens will get the picture. For instance, you can photograph almost the entire interior of a room with a 28mm lens when the normal 50mm lens would give you less than half of it; or you can concentrate on a person's face in a crowded room and show at the same time the relationship of that face to all the others around it including the background or general environment; or you can get the church and all of its steeple from as close as across the street; or you can capture the broad scenic view instead of only a part of it. In short, with even a medium wide-angle lens (28mm or 35mm) you can take the wide picture or the tall picture from a close-in position.

No less useful a feature of the wide-angle lens is its great depth-of-field. Because its range of sharpness is so extensive, it is unnecessary to focus on the subject with anything like the care needed with normal and long lenses. For this reason alone,

Granddaughters and a camera go well together. I introduce them
here to illustrate a use of the medium-long lens, in this case a
135mm. From five feet, this lens enables you to fill the frame with
head and shoulders, and because of its narrow depth-of-field to

make a soft portrait in which no given feature is sharp. Disturbing background is subdued. Available light lends its own quality to the pictures.

Available light and a 135mm lens fill the frame with soft detail.

The value of a good lens can be seen in this picture of a 250-year-old tavern which is now being restored. As much detail as possible was needed and the lens recorded it all from a distance of 40 feet. Every brick and shingle is sharply delineated by the 50mm lens.

The same 50mm lens performed equally well in getting these pictures of interesting locks. Taken from 2½ feet with a bright, low-angle sun shining, the details of the locks' surfaces stand out sharply. Close focusing brought out such details as the skull and crossbones of the pirate's lock and the insignia of Queen Victoria (the crown and VR, for Victoria Regina) on the keyhole cover of a lock that once secured the Queen's stables.

when I sling my camera over my shoulder and go somewhere without having in mind any particular photographic intent, the lens on the camera is my wide-angle 28mm because I know that no matter what opportunity arises I can throw the camera to my eye with reasonable assurance that the taken photo will be acceptably sharp from foreground to background. As the writer-photographer acquires experience, all he has to do in a quick-shooting situation when a wide-angle lens is on his camera is to set the distance ring on the lens to the estimated distance and not bother to focus through the viewfinder. The range of error is so small as to be negligible, or he can pre-set and leave the ring setting at 15 feet and the diaphragm opening at f/11 (an average opening) and know that everything will be in sharp focus from 10 feet in front of the camera all the way to infinity.

Again a logical question might be asked. Since the wide-angle lens and the long lens appear as a team to be able to care for just about all photographic needs, why have a normal or general purpose lens such as the 50mm? The best answer is, I think, that the middle range of lenses (50mm to 58mm) gives you, as a general rule, faster lenses than the wide-angle and long lenses, and there are numerous occasions when only the fast lens will get the picture.

It is best right here to define the word, fast, as it is concerned with lenses so that you will not get the wrong impression. It has nothing to do with speed. The same word is used to describe the shutter of your camera, in which case it is used to mean speed in terms of seconds and their fractions. A fast shutter, for instance, might operate at $\frac{1}{1000}$ of a second. When used to describe a lens, fast is a relative term referring to the amount of light that the diaphragm opening is capable of transmitting to the film. Thus, one lens is twice as fast as another if it can feed twice as much light to the film or, in other words, if its diaphragm opening is twice as large.

A fast lens is invaluable for the writer-photographer in all low-light situations when he cannot or does not choose to use

A sharp 50mm lens focused closely brings out the fine details of carpentry done more than 200 years ago and today. The elaborate window frame over the door is old; the door itself is old except for one frame member and two of the panels. Can you spot the reconstructed parts?

flash equipment. Many a photographer loves to take pictures by available light, as I do, and when there is little light he will get the shot with his fast lens knowing that his wide-angle or long lenses can not get it.

From this general discussion of lenses, I hope the writer will see the need when he gets into photography of having a wide-angle, a normal and a long lens. He need not acquire them all at once. Perhaps he can take a leaf from my book, and, starting with the normal lens on his SLR, take and sell enough pictures with his stories to pay for first a wide-angle lens and then for a medium long lens. One of each is all he will ever need. In this connection, I have recommendations to make about the choice of lenses for practical picture taking.

Beginning with the wide-angles, which range from 15mm to 35mm, my choice would be the 28mm, a moderate wide-angle lens that has so far met all of my own requirements in picture taking. For the writer-photographer, I cannot see the need for anything more extreme than this one. My second choice would be the 35mm, a lens that is often preferred by professional photographers as their normal lens. Although its lateral range is not as great as that of the 28mm, it is still considerably wider than what the normal lens gives you and, of course, provides greater depth-of-field than the 50mm. The 35mm can also be had these days in a version that is just as fast as a normal lens, so that, if you cared to, you could eliminate the normal lens and use the fast 35mm for wide-angle and normal lens photography. I think, however, that a battery of three lenses will give you more capability.

In the normal lens group which can be considered for our purposes as ranging from above the 35mm to the 58mm, I like the 50mm. I use a Nikon camera and Nikon Nikkor lenses, a combination that I have no fault with, and my 50mm, which came with the camera as the normal lens, is as fast a lens as I shall ever need (f/1.4). Lately, I have been plagued by the itch to turn this lens in for one of the fast 35 mm lenses, a condition that afflicts the photographer from time to time, but the more I think about it the more convinced I am that I am better off as things stand.

The medium long lens group includes the 85mm, the 105mm, the 135mm and the 180mm. The many others in the telephoto class are not considered here because they are for highly specialized uses (as is the case also for the extreme wide-angle lenses) and the writer-photographer would simply be wasting his money if he bought one. My choice is the 135mm. This lens, it seems to me, is a better choice in this group than any of the others because it has the capability to do the long-lens job better than the 85mm and the 105mm, and can be held to the eye more steadily than the 180mm which weighs almost three times more.

My lens equipment, then, consists of a 28mm, a 50mm and a 135mm, and since they have served me so well, I can suggest them to you as good choices. The professional who sets off to cover a big photographic assignment will take with him several cameras and a dozen or more lenses—hundreds of pounds of equipment. The writer-photographer has no need for all that. My camera case holding lenses, camera, film, lens hoods, filters and flash equipment weighs nine pounds.

Assuming that you have an SLR camera at hand, it would be worthwhile to examine the lens, no matter what lens it is, in order to understand its operation and the markings on the barrel that refer to its capabilities. In addition, you will come to realize what a marvelous mechanism it is, and, perhaps, to know why it costs as much as it does. It's been said before that a camera is no better than the man who is using it. It must be said now that it is no better than its lens.

Looking into the lens, you can see the diaphragm which one writer has described as looking like "a bunch of razor blades fastened in a circle." Like the iris of the eye, the diaphragm opens or closes to admit more or less light. In the eye, this action is automatic; in the photographic lens, it is controlled by a lever or a turning ring and is set by hand for the exposure desired. A set of numbers on the barrel of the lens indicates the various degrees to which the diaphragm can be opened or closed. These numbers are f/-numbers or f/-stops (f/ being the abbreviation for focal). The larger the f/-number, the smaller the diaphragm opening, and the smaller the number, the larger the opening. Lenses are designated by their largest opening. The f/-numbers are derived by dividing the focal length of the lens by the diameter. Thus, a lens which is 2 inches in focal length and 1 inch in diameter is designated as an f/2 lens; and a lens of the same length but with a diameter of ½ inch would be an f/4 lens (2 divided by ½).

Without going any deeper into technicalities that only tend to confuse, it can be said that when your lens barrel has f/-numbers such as 2–2.8–4–5.6–8–11–16—the largest number (16) indicates the smallest opening, which admits half as much light as the next numbered opening in descending order (11), which in turn admits half as much as the next opening (8), and so on down to the 2 opening, which is the full open position of the lens. Of course, the reverse is true also—the 2 opening admits twice as much light as the 2.8 opening, and so on. You can see the opening in the diaphragm double or halve itself as you turn the ring or lever from one setting to the next.

The barrel of the lens also carries another set of numbers marked in feet or meters or both which indicate the distance settings of the lens. The lens can be turned in or out to any setting ranging from infinity (lens all the way in) to the closest capability of the given lens—2 feet or 5 feet or whatever—(lens all the way out). You can bring your subject into focus either by viewing it through the finder and turning the focusing ring until the subject appears sharp, or by estimating the distance and setting the ring at the appropriate figure. In the latter instance, however, you would either have to consult a depth-of-field chart for the lens being used in order to be sure that the subject was in the area of sharpness, or you would have to know from experience what the capabilities are of the lens with respect to depth-of-field. Because it is all but impossible to remember accurately what these figures are, the manufacturers indicate depth-of-field ranges on the barrel of the lens in conjunction with the distance settings. On the Nikkor lenses, for instance, the f/-numbers are color coded to the depth-of-field ranges, so that the photographer can tell at a glance what the general range of sharpness is for each diaphragm setting. For example, when using the 50mm lens set at infinity and at the f/16 opening (blue) the range of sharpness is from infinity (blue line at left on barrel) to 15 feet (blue line at right on barrel). When set at 15 feet at f/8 (pink) the range of sharpness is indicated by the pink line at the left as about 28 feet and by the pink line at the right as about 11 feet.

Although such settings and indicators on the lens barrel are not as accurate as the calculated figures used in depth-of-field charts, they are close enough for most picture taking. Obviously, when the need is critical, the chart for the given lens should be consulted. But you will find little need to do this unless the subject is very close to the camera and is third dimensional, and the lens you are using is naturally short on depth-of-field.

The more you become acquainted with your lenses and what they can do the better you can manipulate them to achieve desired effects. Although, in general, sharp pictures are desirable, there are times when your purpose will be to produce a mood or atmosphere photograph. Such an instance occurred once when I was writing an article for the *Philadelphia Bulletin* Sunday magazine supplement and will illustrate the point. The subject was a 200-year-old graveyard. In photographing the scene, I wanted to create an eerie illusion if I could. Using a 50mm lens with the diaphragm almost wide open, I got a print that was out of focus enough in the middle and far distances to cause the gravestones, which were leaning in all directions, and the trees in the background to have a slightly fuzzy appearance. The effect when printed in the paper was even more illusory, with little definition and an overall quality of softness. My purpose here was aided by the day itself which was cloudy and overcast so that there was little or no shadow or contrast, lending a kind of flat paleness to the picture. If this scene had been sharply in focus, as when taken with a wide-angle lens, the picture would have been no more than a factual statement, rather than the suggestion of a possibility.

Thus, to know what a given lens can do is to enable you to suit your pictures to the mood of the story, if the mood is well enough defined to warrant the effort.

We come now to another element in photography, in addition to the camera body and the lens you use with it—and that is the kind of film you work with. Here, as in the case of lenses, use of the word, fast, comes into play. Films are categorized in general as slow, fast and very fast, and designated by an ASA rating established by the American Standards Association in order to make comparisons possible. With films, speed is associated with sensitivity to light—the more sensitive the film, the faster. Thus, it is clear that the faster the film or the more sensitive it is to light, the better that film is to get pictures in low-light situations. On the other hand, when using a fast film in bright sunlight, its high sensitivity forces the use of small diaphragm openings and fast shutter speeds. Accordingly, light conditions generally dictate what film to use.

For the purposes of the writer-photographer, it is totally unnecessary to consider the use of other than Kodak's Plus-X or Tri-X films or their equivalents made by other manufacturers. They have been satisfactory for me, and since I have not felt the need to experiment with other makes or speeds, as perhaps the photojournalist might, or the dedicated hobbyist, I have stuck with these two Kodak films. As a matter of interest, when I was starting out in photography, a staff photographer for the *Philadelphia Bulletin* advised me to use Plus-X all of the time and to forget about anything faster. I followed that advice for a long time, but then found that occasions arose when Tri-X, which is much more sensitive, was necessary. So I carry and use both as needed. The index rating for Plus-X is ASA 125, and for Tri-X is ASA 400, as marked on the film package, but their range of sensitivity is even greater, and the settings for these films on your camera can be adjusted to care for this if you choose to use the faster ratings.

It is appropriate when discussing film to bring up the matter of processing the negative and making prints. When you have a roll of exposed film in your hand, you have three choices: take the film to a commercial photofinisher via the drugstore, the camera shop or some other outlet for his services; take it to a custom photofinisher; or do the work yourself in your own darkroom. From the first source, you will get the run-of-the-mill job, with no attention paid at all to the possibilities that exist in your negative, and from the custom man you will get excellent prints but you will pay for them. Having your own darkroom is something else again—the question is whether or not to get into your own photofinishing at all.

I look at this question from several angles. As a freelancer with a regular job, I don't have all the time in the world. Digging out the story, writing it and getting pictures take all the spare time available to me. If I set up a darkroom, I'd be spending more time on developing and printing and less on writing and photography, which in the end would defeat my purpose.

From the point of view of expense, there would be considerable outlay at the beginning for a good enlarger and other equipment, but this would be made up for in the long run.

From the fun angle, I can see a certain fascination in having a darkroom, but I have enough fun as it is with my typewriter and camera.

All-in-all, I'd rather rely first on my darkroom friend, mentioned in an earlier chapter, whose skills in photofinishing are superb, and, second, on a custom shop where they'll do what I want them to. You'll have to decide for yourself, considering the time you have available, and the money, and, most of all, where your real interests lie.

7

The Market–And
How To Make One Subject
Do Double Duty

One of the most baffling problems that faces the beginning writer-photographer, and sometimes the more experienced, too, is that of finding the right outlet for his work. The problem disappears almost altogether as one gains experience—and rejections—followed by an occasional acceptance and then a steady flow. If anything is at all certain, it is that the writer's best effort is now and then turned down by the very publication that had taken his last six pieces. This is a blow to the ego at most, and is temporary; but the writer by now knows enough not to worry about it for long—he sends the story to the next best bet on his list. Eventually, he may have the satisfaction, one that I have been fortunate to feel a few times, of having an editor write, saying that he saw your story in such and such a paper or magazine and why the devil hadn't you sent it to him instead. It is nice to be wanted.

The market for the writer-photographer is big. Like that of television, its maw is bottomless, digesting each day tons of paper and pictures offered to it by thousands of writers and photographers. If anything can be lovely about a bottomless maw, it is that it must be fed every day, thus offering continuous hope and promises to those writer-photographers who have more to give than mere lip service to the desire to produce illustrated stories. In short, if you have ability and work at it, the market is there waiting for your product.

Mainly, the market for your work is newspapers and magazines. From the local weekly newspaper to the great-city dailies of which some are really national in character and influence and have wide distribution, the range of opportunity is staggering. You have to narrow it down, at least until your experience strengthens, to those papers that you know best, starting perhaps by submitting something to your local weekly or daily, then edging up to the county or state-wide paper, which might include that of the largest city in the state. When—not if—you succeed in these areas, you can shoot at the nationally known papers. To aim at the top before you're ready for it, is really foolish unless, of course, you are a genius. Your immaturity will show through your work, and no kind of editor in the world is more able to spot your faults than the hard-bitten (said kindly) department editor of a big newspaper. It is better to build from the bottom. As a consequence, your experience and confidence grow, and acceptances will come more regularly.

With magazines, or other periodicals, the rate of consumption is slower, but there are so many of them in so many varied fields of interest that there is a constant need for good material. This market has to be studied more carefully than the newspaper market because you have to fit the peg to the hole—the subject of your story and pictures must fit the nature of the magazine, or else your effort is no-go.

In connection with the newspaper and periodical market, it has been my habit for years to use *Writer's Market*, an annual published by Writer's Digest, Cincinnati, Ohio, which lists magazines of all sorts and the Sunday supplements of newspapers, all of which are looking for good article and picture material. Names and addresses are included, as well as a brief description of the kind of material each publication uses. This is an invaluable tool for any writer-photographer.

In addition to newspapers and magazines, a lucrative field for your work is the house organ, a somewhat sonorous name for what is no more than a company or firm periodical. There are two kinds of house organ, internal and external, the former being the little sheet put out by someone within an organization for the consumption of the employees, and featuring in general a message from management of some uplifting sort and a collection of personal notes relating to employee marriages and other activities. You can forget the internal house organ which doesn't take outside stuff because it is produced entirely by the girls in the office.

On the other hand, you must not forget the external house organ, which is something else again. More than 5,000 companies publish them with the general intent to establish and maintain good public and customer relations. Most will go out of their way to find good feature articles with photographs on subjects of general interest, and they pay very well, sometimes as much as or more than a magazine will. If you can find a good connection with an external house organ, it will be worthwhile. In this field for the writer-photographer, I have been very lucky over the past twenty years, having been in my spare time the exclusive producer of hundreds of issues spread among five house organs concerned with the printing industry—*The Graphic Artery, The Hellbox, Impressions, Inklings,* and *The Printed Page.* (It is of interest, I think, in this connection, to note that only a month ago, as this page is written, a total stranger phoned me to ask if I was the John Milton who used to write *The Graphic Artery* years ago. He asked if I would consider writing and producing a similar publication for his firm. I had to decline—too busy as it is; but I confess to feeling a faint glow of sinful pride at having been remembered.)

The market, then, is wide and long and receptive; and because the material is used up so quickly and new readers are always coming along, it is possible, not to say probable, to see in a current issue of any given publication a story based on a subject that had been written about in the same publication a year or so before. The market seems to open again for similar stories every twelve months or so.

I learned about this the hard way. The travel editor of *The New York Times* had accepted an article I had done on the colonial Corbit house in Odessa, Delaware. Then, the whole thing came back with the following letter.'

May 12, 1966

Dear Mr. Milton:

This is a nice piece you have on Odessa and I was about to take it on, so much so that I started editing it until one of my men pointed out that we had a story on this same town only last fall, which makes it too soon for us to do it again. I'm sorry.

You have a nice, clean manuscript to peddle somewhere else—I had your manuscript copied. Since I have no use for it, I am enclosing the original as well along with your photographs. Anything else in the works for us?

Sincerely,
P. J. C. F.
Editor

This was my first experience with what we can call the rejection of an acceptance according to the calendar. But, I had a second four years later with the same paper but a different editor. His letter tells it all.

August 11, 1970

Dear Mr. Milton:

I am sorry to report that I cannot, after all, use your most interesting piece about Fortress Louisbourg in Nova Scotia. A colleague, who liked your article very much and accepted it during my absence on vacation, did not realize that a piece on the same topic was published in the Travel Section last September. Regretfully, I am returning your manuscript. However, I should be interested to hear from you on any other ideas you may have for contributions to the section.

Sincerely,
R. W. S.
Editor

Despite an almost constant drizzle mixed with touches of fog, the lens was able to pick up the fine detail of wood and stone in this facade of Fortress Louisbourg in Nova Scotia.

If either of these articles had reached the *Times* a few months later, it would have been published. I wondered at the time why the editor didn't keep the articles and use them when he could, but I soon realized that, for one thing, they had a seasonal flavor to them, and to use them at all would have meant holding them for nearly a year. There might be something, too, in what the first editor said about retyping the edited piece so that I could "peddle" it somewhere else.

As it turned out in the case of the Louisbourg article, I had no need to peddle it anywhere. I simply used more of my material, enlarged upon the theme, and the story was published in an issue of *The Printed Page*. The Odessa story was not peddled either—it reposes in my dead file as something to do something with sometime.

These two experiences taught me something that I have put to use a number of times, and you might consider it for whatever value it has in your own work. On the basis of the same material, it is possible to write two articles for different publications; that is, you can make the same material do double duty and produce double income. I do not want to mislead you in this matter. You can't produce strongly similar pieces and submit them to the same kind of publication (two newspapers or two magazines) at the same time. I am not advocating this. I am saying that you can write a newspaper article on a given topic, and then, using the same source material, write in greater depth for publication in a magazine or house organ. In other words, all of your labor in researching and photographing a subject need not be killed off by a single writing effort. The nature of the market gives you latitude in this respect, and with proper attention to putting the second piece together, you can publish it ethically and legitimately.

Proper attention means writing the second, in-depth story from scratch with not so much as a single sentence extracted

When far from home base, you take pictures of everything. Here are dungeons inside the inner wall of the King's Bastion.

A natural shot of the Fortress's gateway from the inside. No photographer would miss its detail.

whole from the first story; it means expansion of the story through use of more facts and greater detail, and not through use of more words in an effort to pad; and it means using photographs that were not published with the first story.

Here, it is important to emphasize something said earlier—that it is wise when gathering information and taking pictures to do a thorough job of it, even though at the time you may think that you have too much material and too many photos for use in the immediate job.

Working on this principle of having plenty of material, I have had a number of features on the same subject published in newspapers first, and then in magazines or house organs. Perhaps I lean over backward too much—but, if I do, it has the effect of making everything clear: I always let the editor of the magazine or house organ know that a story of mine on the same topic appeared first in a newspaper.

As you become familiar with the market in general and your stories and pictures are accepted in one or more of its numerous and varied areas, you will find yourself, I think, leaning toward specific kinds of publications—trade journals, let us say, as opposed to consumer publications, specific as opposed to the general. This is likely to come about because your basic interests by their very nature will channel you one way or another. It is the case of water seeking its own level. I know writer-photographers who work exclusively in technical areas and wouldn't think for a moment of trying anything else because it doesn't interest them; and I know others who wouldn't touch a trade journal job for the same reason even if handed an assignment. Accordingly, your underlying interests, knowledge, training, education and enthusiasms will determine your course.

8

How To Know
What Editors Want

The editor of a magazine that is devoted to the interests of fishermen is hardly likely to look kindly on an article submitted to him that deals with dairying or crocheting. A magazine whose readership is composed of electronic engineers won't go for a story concerned with dune buggies. The writer is writing for a specific kind of audience and the editor of a publication that reaches that group is, in effect, a middleman serving the group and the writer. If you look at it this way, you will see that the more you know about a publication's readership, the better able you will be to satisfy the editor's need for suitable material. Editors want what readers want.

The obvious road to acceptance, then, is through an understanding of what magazine reaches what group, or what group reads what magazine. From my point of view, all outlets for written material can be split into two broad groups encompassing magazines and newspapers. One is aimed at people who have special interests, and the other at those who have general interests. In the special interest group, we find trade magazines that appeal to people in all areas of business and industry according to the work they do. A few newspapers fit the category, too, in one way or another. For instance, *Variety* interests people in show business; *The Wall Street Journal* is read by those concerned with business and finance. Other newspapers are allied with special groups in the sense that they are Republican or Democratic newspapers. Apart from the trade magazines, other periodicals are written for children (surely a special group), for photographers, for parents, for sailors—for hundreds and hundreds of different groups, each with its own special needs.

In the general interest area are publications that are read by everybody and anybody—the mass circulation periodicals. Their readers are not likely to be looking for more than light entertainment—something to help pass the time away.

In either case, specific or general, editorial needs change with much the same regularity that seems to govern fashion. It would appear, if one were to watch a single publication over a year or two, that editors fear anything that tends to stereotype their publications too rigidly—anything that casts them into so rigid a mold that it would be difficult to meet changing tastes. Ever conscious of his readers, his advertisers and the fickle quality of changing times, the editor looks for material that will label his publication modern and progressive, and the leader in its field.

Thus, the writer-photographer must know something of the current trend of the publication to which he intends to submit material, and the more he knows about a given publication and its readers, the more able he will be to satisfy the requirements of its editor. This knowledge can be acquired in at least two ways, one of which is to keep at hand for reference the annual issue of *Writer's Market*, mentioned earlier, which describes in good detail what editors are looking for. Since trends do not occur suddenly or with calculated regularity, but emerge gradually, the likelihood is that what that book has to say about the kind of material being accepted is correct.

The second way to get a line on what interests a publication is through personal observation. Get copies of the publications that cover your fields of interest. Study the articles. Are they long or short? Do they take in-depth material? Do they ever permit writers to use the first person in writing? Do they go for bright writing (when it can be achieved not too obtrusively) or do they rely on straightforward, factual material only?

From this kind of objective look at the vehicle itself, you can soon decide whether on not what you have written or intend to write will have a chance of acceptance; and the more able you are to tailor the piece to the publication, the more success in getting stories published.

Two instances in my own experience with changing trends occur to me. I mention them here for what they are worth. One is concerned with the travel section of *The New York Times;* the other with the Sunday magazine supplement of the *Philadelphia Bulletin.* When I began writing stories for the *Times* some years ago, almost every issue ran stories by various writers ranging from 1,000 to 1,500 words. Now, stories in this paper range into the many thousands of words and cover one or more pages, and the shorter pieces are seldom used. The shorter, factual, third person pieces have given way to the in-depth, first person, personal experience kind of article. It is to be noted in this connection that this change occurred soon after a new editor came on the scene. A change in editors or in editorial policy is an internal thing, and it therefore is incumbent on you, the writer-photographer, to keep an observant eye on the publications you write for, or want to write for, with a view toward meeting their needs of the moment.

The direction of change at the *Bulletin* was even more radical. For years, ever since its inception in fact, the magazine used feature articles of 1,500 words and up about interesting occupations or personalities drawn from the large Philadelphia city and suburban area. Almost suddenly, editorial policy changed (a notice of the fact was sent to me by the editor) and the magazine turned away from human interest pieces to articles about home-making, decorating, food and the like. Unlike the change at the *Times,* which was one of style, the change at the *Bulletin* was one of content and character.

In both connections, it seems not unlikely to see sooner or later, another change, either back to the old way or in some new direction, for neither of these publications can be static.

Getting to know what an editor wants can develop after a time into something more positive than merely studying current issues of publications and referring to *Writer's Market*. It happens, however, only after you have been accepted a few times and your name becomes familiar to the editor. My experience in this respect is both good and bad, but by telling of it here you may be able to benefit by avoiding a pitfall into which I fell head first.

First the good part. With the *Bulletin*, I began by submitting a number of short shorts—little pieces of 200 words or so, vignettes with touches of humor. Most were published. Then, from my point-of-view, a curious, hopeful and happy event occurred. The assistant editor sent a note to the editor who sent it on to me with a scribbled message to "come in and have a talk." The assistant editor (a wonderful fellow) liked my writing and suggested to the editor that it would be nice if they could get a longer piece out of me. I had that talk with the editor and learned firsthand what kind of articles they were interested in. From then on, I provided a steady stream of them, and it was a very happy connection.

One of my ideas for a story at the time illustrates to what extent an editor will go to get what he wants. I suggested that I ride around a rural free delivery route with a mailman and write about the experience. The editor said that was fine with him, but that he thought it was illegal for anyone to ride with a mailman, which turned out to be true. Undaunted, he got off a letter to the paper's correspondent in Washington, D.C., who, in turn, obtained written permission from the Post Office Department—and arrangements were made for me to ride with a selected mailman while he covered his 400-mailbox territory. It was a good story that evoked much interest, particularly among the people along his route. An editor with less on the ball might not have followed through. (See more about this story in Chapter 11.)

With the *Times*, I began with a piece that I had given up on four years earlier and then resurrected, as described in the

Preface. After several other articles had been published and my name and work were better known to the editor, I had a phone call from him one day. He asked if I would accept an assignment. Mustering as much aplomb as I could, although I was partly in shock, I agreed to get the story he wanted, which, he said, was in my "territory" and only 75 miles away. It seems that the Department of Development (tourist) of the State of Maryland had suggested to the *Times* that an article should be written about old Linchester Mill at Preston, Maryland. The editor wanted this story in a hurry. I covered it, and from time to time the editor gave me other assignments. Admittedly, to get assignments like these was a chance thing for me, but it sprang out of the editor's confidence in my earlier work.

So much for the good part in working with editors and knowing something about what they want. The bad part—the pitfall—happened with the *Times*, and it has a bearing on what to do and what not to do in dealing with an editor. I learned from this and have not fallen into the same trap.

It begins with a note from the editor which said, "What else have you got for us?" Full of ideas, I sent him a list of 15 subjects worthy of articles that would interest *Times* readers, and brief descriptions of each. He selected one of the 15, and the story was written and published. But, in selecting one, the editor was, in effect, rejecting the other 14 as possibilities. In spilling out all those lovely ideas on his desk at one time, I had effectively killed off all but one as *Times* material. This was at the time another kind of shock—a painful one—but I managed to recover and did get 10 of the rejected story-ideas into print in other publications. I am convinced that if I had submitted one idea after another most would have been accepted by the *Times*. I had simply overwhelmed the poor editor. Actually, over the next 24 months, several articles did appear in that paper on those rejected subjects, but written by other writers. This would seem to imply that what is unacceptable at one time is acceptable at another. So—don't submit more than one story-idea at a time. The editor can't and won't favor all of them.

Another matter related to editors and what they want is concerned with sending a query asking if a story on a certain subject would be of interest. As an editor of books in my daily work, I have some thoughts about this that might be helpful.

In general, it is a waste of time for the writer to send a query and a waste of time for the editor to deal with it. The occasional success with this approach is overwhelmed by the many failures. Your query, consisting of a few lines describing your story-idea, and the question, "Would you be interested in 1,500 to 2,000 words on this subject?", requires that he think about the idea for a moment, that he make up his mind about it, that he write to tell you to go ahead with it or forget it. With all the other details of his job on his mind, he is likely, not to say inclined, to thrust the query aside and forget it himself. After all, he has a stack of manuscripts on hand already and they need attention. They are accomplished facts—they are real—and your query is simply a suggestion. So, the editor will probably take up first things first—and you, the anxious writer-photographer, will wait—and wait—and wait. You may never hear about your story-idea at all.

On the other hand, suppose that you send the story itself and the pictures to go with it, including return postage. It reaches the editor's hands. In a few moments he is able to tell whether or not it is something he wants. He can judge the package as something real and finished and ready. There is no doubt in his mind about your ability to follow through on a query, for what he has before him is solid proof. He will take it or not, based on quality and his need for it. If he takes it, you'll hear from him quickly. If he doesn't, you'll soon get your material back and can send it somewhere else. In either event, you will know the answer and won't waste your time waiting.

It seems to me to be the smart thing to give the editor as little trouble as possible. Make it easy for him by giving him what he really wants—which, of course, is the complete job. He'd rather have one manuscript to judge than two queries to wonder about.

Since there is always an exception to everything, there is one here, too. Once you become known to a given editor who has published your stories and articles, it is possible to write or phone him about a story suggestion, and come away from it with a go-ahead. But, when this happens, you can be sure that it is only because he has confidence in your ability to follow through—confidence based on past performance. Until that happy circumstance, don't send queries.

You have heard it said that editors are always looking for good material to publish. This is true. If your rejections pile up, it is not because the editor is capricious—it is because your material is not good enough for him, or because he is already overloaded with good stories and can't take on any more at the moment. This is true also—that any editor who finds a good writer-photographer is anxious to get more material from him. As a consequence of this fact, it is wise, when your story or article is accepted, to come right back with another. Strike while the iron is hot.

One of the most pleasing notes that I ever received from an editor consisted of three handwritten words in rough pencil—"Keep 'em coming."

9

How To Help The Editor
To Like Your Work

Loosely speaking, the difference between the professional and the amateur in many areas of endeavor, sports for instance, is that the former is paid for his work and the latter does it for love. An editor friend of mine once mentioned to me that I was a professional when he learned that I had sold some pictures for publication. On this basis, I have never felt that I qualified for the designation, since I did not make my living by selling photographs. In this sense, I was possibly a semi-pro. Whether or not play-for-pay is the criterion for professionalism in the general view, my own definition is contrary to it. I think that a professional, in any area, is one who does a workmanlike job, and that, conversely, an amateur is one who does not. The word, amateur, in general parlance implies a lack of professionalism. Obviously, the professional is likely to be paid for his work.

You, the writer-photographer, will be able to shrug off the weaknesses of the amateur and become a professional in proportion to the attention you give to workmanship. The shoddier the job you do, the more obvious your lack of professionalism to the editor. He is a professional and he likes to deal with professionals. However, even though you are a beginner (as opposed to amateur), you can influence the editor by acting like a pro. He judges you on the basis of your work and the manner in which you present it.

The professional way to submit written material is grounded

on common sense. The reasons are plain. The overriding rule is—be thorough, do the whole job with care and consideration, pay attention to details. Here is a checklist of details worth paying attention to.

1. Type double-space on a good grade of white paper, leaving at least an inch of margin at both sides. The margins are for editorial notations as is the space between lines.

2. Put your name and address at the upper left corner of the first page only, and the word count of the piece at the upper right corner. Number each page at the upper right. On the second and following pages, put your last name only at the upper left. With your name on each page, there is no chance of a mix-up between two manuscripts. The word count tells the editor how much space your story will need; without it, he'd be forced to estimate it, an event to be avoided.

3. Put the title of the piece half-way down from the top of the first page, or a little above that, and begin the body of the copy (text) three or four lines below the title. Leave about an inch of space at the bottom of the page. On the second and following pages, begin about an inch from the top and observe the rule for margins.

4. It is unnecessary to clip the pages together, but it won't be held against you if you use a paper clip (why throw it away?). Never staple the pages.

5. Your manuscript should be typed neatly and be appealing to read. No editor minds an occasional correction of the type-written matter, done by ballpoint (never pencil) if that correction consists of only a word or two. He will be turned off, if you will pardon the expression, by heavy re-writing or editing, overuse of underlining (which would be set in italic in the printed piece), and by any other messing up of the page. If you should find on re-reading your story that any substantial changes must be made, re-type the material—don't attempt to save time and effort by writing it in by hand. To delete a word, simply draw a line through it—don't obliterate it or slash it

from the page. Never paste a new piece of text over an old piece—and if you ever resort to Scotch tape you deserve rejection on the spot. Neatness counts.

6. Give your material a final check. Read it for errors in typing and spelling. If in doubt about a word, look it up and spell it right. Punctuate on the basis of reason and good sense. Be consistent. In your final reading for the sense of the story try to anticipate any question that the editor or the reader might be inclined to ask, and give the answer first.

7. Don't make the silly mistake. This area in particular will quickly reveal unprofessional lack of care. Don't let the editor get the feeling that you don't care—if you don't care, he won't care either. Silly mistakes include pages out of numerical order, failure to number pages or a page, finger-smudged pages, missing pages, failure to include return postage and self-addressed return envelope, bad packaging.

Since you will be submitting photographs along with your story, particular attention must be given to their handling. You will be sending at least six pictures so that the editor can have a choice. The editor will be predisposed toward you and them if you send 8 by 10 glossy prints, but will not reject 5 by 7 prints, or mat (dull finish) prints if they are especially sharp. Here's how to submit your photographs.

1. On a single sheet of white paper, type the legends for all six pictures. These legends identify the pictures, describe what they are and otherwise characterize them. Don't attempt to do more than that. The editor is going to rewrite them to suit himself anyway. What he wants to know is what the picture is all about. All you need is a sentence or two.

2. Cut each legend from the sheet of paper and paste it down on the back of the appropriate picture at the bottom, using rubber cement. Be sure to rub away any excess cement so that one picture will not stick to another. Put your name and address on the back of each picture, using a rubber stamp if you have one, or failing in that, using crayon or a ballpoint

pen very lightly in order not to indent the emulsion on the
face of the print. This would leave marks in the printed picture
if the editor ever let it get by him.

3. Package the photos for mailing by sandwiching them
between two 8 by 10 (or slightly larger) pieces of cardboard,
and use two rubber bands, one up and down and the other
across, to hold the package securely. Never use a paper clip to
hold the pictures together or to clip anything to them—this
would dent the emulsion and possibly ruin the picture.

4. You now have a manuscript and a packet of pictures.
Slip them all into an envelope that is slightly larger than the
manuscript page, which is $8\frac{1}{2}$ by 11. Include a self-addressed
envelope of the same size (fold it once) and clip (do not paste)
enough postage to it to ensure its return if necessary. I have
found it highly convenient in this connection to have a rubber
stamp of my name and address and a small post-office-approved
weighing scale at hand. The scale, in particular, lets you complete the package at home, whereas if you have to take it to
the post office to determine the correct postage you will have
to leave the package unsealed so that you can insert the return
postage in the mailing envelope before dropping the package
into the box. Mail your material first class.

Almost every beginner is tempted to include a note or letter
in his package to the publication. If he lets his emotions sway
his judgment, he will write a little message to the editor
expressing his hopes for the story, or giving an explanation,
or even offering a small apology of some sort ("I'm sorry if
the story is too short, but I can add to it.") He feels, perhaps,
that such a note will help to establish a connection with the
editor—a person-to-person relationship. What the writer should
do is to let his manuscript and pictures—his work—stand for
itself without benefit of notes or letters. No personal message
to the editor is going to change his evaluation of your work
or affect it in the slightest degree. He will make no concessions
because your note to him said that you had written your story
with one hand because the other was in a cast. What he is

interested in is the job itself, not in how, where or why you did it. His look at your work has to be subjective and any ploy, whether undertaken consciously or unconsciously, will serve only to annoy and irritate. If there is to be any closer, more personal relationship with an editor in a business way, let it begin with and come from the editorial side. When that happens, it is because your work was impressive and whatever might follow is all to the good—your good.

The time may come when the editor will want to know something of your personal history and background so that he can write a thumbnail sketch of you as a writer—some identifying paragraph that would interest readers. Instead of offering such information, let the editor ask for it.

In general, you can help the editor to like your work by playing it cool, staying in the background, letting your words and pictures do the talking. All you really have to do to understand the editor's position and viewpoint is to ask yourself the question, "What would I want if I were the editor?"

10

The Writer-Photographer And The IRS

You may hold a full-time salaried job, but if you do freelance writing and photography in your spare time you are also self-employed, a condition in life that guarantees certain benefits not given to those who work simply for salary or wages. You are lumped in with the farmer and the small businessman—if you spend money in the pursuit of income, you can deduct it from your taxable income. You are concerned with profit and loss, and are entitled to what the tax laws provide. In essence, those laws permit you to deduct the costs of producing income. If, at the end of a year's work, your costs exceed your income, your tax return would show a loss; and you'd have a profit if you brought in more than you paid out.

The more you know about all this, the more able you will be to use the self-employment tax laws to your advantage and to turn a loss into a profit. Ignorance hurts you, not the IRS. My own ignorance in this regard years ago burned my pocketbook in the first year of my freelance work. I earned some writing fees and reported this income along with my regular salary, but I knew nothing about deducting expenses incurred. I learned the facts from a fellow freelancer, quite by accident, and from then on I did justice to myself—I engaged the services of an accountant who handled the tax matters of a number of farmers and storekeepers. For a small annual fee, he has made out my tax papers ever since at a considerable saving to me. However, his work is limited by and contingent upon the information I give him. In my case, and in yours, it is necessary to prepare complete lists of expenses, income and other supporting data, and to work with a tax accountant who can handle all the nasty, sticky details with ease and accuracy, and with satisfaction to both yourself and the IRS. I would advise the use of a tax accountant who knows the problems peculiar to the self-employed—not just some hole-in-the-wall, self-styled tax expert who sets up shop from January 1 to April 15 and then goes back to plumbing or clerking.

The typical deductible costs of a writer-photographer are more extensive and inclusive than what might at first appear. The supplies you buy are obvious: typing paper, typewriter ribbons, paper clips, postage stamps and envelopes—anything that you use in the preparation of a manuscript; and film and processing—anything that you use to produce finished prints. But what about the typewriter itself, and the camera? These are deductible, too—but, since they are classified as working equipment, they are like the fixtures of the storekeeper and are amortized over a period of years, usually ten; that is, 10% of their cost is deducted each year for ten years. Your car is in this category also if you use it for business travel, but in this instance only a percentage is amortized since it is likely that you do not use it only for business travel. You will have to decide what that proportion is.

Travel cost itself, or a proportion of it, is deductible, depending again on how much is for business. This includes gasoline, bridge and road tolls, lodging, meals, and general upkeep such as washing, greasing and licensing. A prime example of how I use this provision in the law is a combined vacation and business trip that I made a couple of years ago to Nova Scotia. It was a vacation from my job, but it was made with my usual intent to find, if I could, a subject or two worth photographing, researching and writing about. Out of that trip came a lengthy story about Fortress Louisbourg which was published with 15 pictures, and several other possibilities for stories (a backlog of

material) that I expect to get to sometime. The income from
that trip paid for the vacation.

Another, and major, deductible expense that is too important
to be called an "item" is the room in which you do your
work—the study, the workroom, the den, or whatever you
call it that you have set aside as the regular place in your
home (house or apartment) for your business activity. It
corresponds to the storekeeper's place of business, and you can
deduct the cost of its maintenance and upkeep. My own workroom is the fourth bedroom in my house, fitted out as an
office—desk, typewriter, filing cabinets, book shelves, telephone.
You may not be as lucky. Perhaps the space available to you
is part of a working bedroom, if not a whole room; but whatever it is, its cost is deductible. Since my house has seven rooms
and I use one of them for business, I deduct one-seventh of
my costs for operating the whole house—one-seventh of all
bills for heating, electricity, mortgage payments. If you were
to build such a workroom in your basement, the costs of
construction would be deductible on a long-term basis.

In the main, these are the areas of expense for the writer-
photographer and all are necessary in the production of income.
It is not intended to do more here than to point out generalities
—the details vary with a given case and it is in this area that
your accountant comes into his own. Your job with respect
to him is to furnish the facts, and his questions to you when
you present them to him will care for the details. He will
want several lists from you, among them one covering all
income and its sources, and another accounting for expenses
broken down into categories such as office maintenance, supplies
and equipment, travel, automobile. With these lists in hand, as
well as statements of income supplied by your regular employer
and from publications, your tax man can do the proper job
for you.

It is axiomatic, of course, that you must be prepared to
back-up or prove what you claim. It is not the duty or
responsibility of the tax accountant to do more than to justify

his handling of the figures that you give him. Therefore, in your freelance work and travels during the fiscal year, it is incumbent upon you to collect your proof as you go. This is done by means of receipts wherever it is possible to come by them. When it is not possible to get a receipt, as for instance when you throw a quarter into a basket at a toll booth, or when you buy a hotdog for lunch at a roadside stand, your estimate of the expenditure will suffice if it is within reason.

My own system is practical and works for me. I go through my check stubs at the end of the year and pick out all payments made for house and car, including insurance. I list them in categories—heat, phone, electricity, insurance, mortgage, interest and the like. Out-of-pocket payments provide receipts in many cases—hotels and motels, supplies, equipment, services—and these go into a large envelope. Other "proof" of expense is estimated and is acceptable to the IRS on the basis of established tables of experience. For instance, automobile mileage for the year is told by the odometer in your car, and since your car gets 15 miles to the gallon, the cost of gasoline can be established, a proportion of which is charged to your travel expense. This is true also where sales taxes are concerned—persons of a certain income can be expected to pay a certain amount in sales taxes.

Thus, with such facts before you, it is possible in a single evening to make your lists of income and expense for your tax accountant. With all this information at hand and your tax forms standing by to be filled in, you may be tempted to do the job yourself and save the accountant's fee. Don't do it. The fee may come to $25 or maybe $50 depending on the complexity of your own situation—but no matter what it is, the dollars you spend now are worth every penny. (And the fee is deductible.) The ramifications of the tax forms for the self-employed are too tough to be fooled with by the amateur. The chances are great that you would lose far more than the fee through overlooking some legitimate deduction; or perhaps even worse, foul up your return to a degree that would arouse doubts in the mind of the computer and get yourself hauled in for questioning.

In the opening paragraph of this chapter, I mentioned the possibility that costs might exceed income in freelance work. This is most likely to happen with the beginner who does the work but fails to get it published, or who tries a dozen times and succeeds but once or twice. He has made sincere efforts to sell his material and has run up solid expenses. Such expenses are, nonetheless, valid losses incurred in the attempt to produce income. I recall with sharp clarity one or two years in my early experience when income from writing amounted to only a hundred dollars or so and expenses ran several times higher. I operated at a loss and reported a loss. The IRS understands sincere efforts to make money, but it won't go along with failures over too long a time. It hopes, one has to suppose, that the writer-photographer or the businessman who cannot learn how to profit from his work will soon go out of business or turn his hand to something else—such as a steady job.

On the other hand, in successful years, the writer-photographer is likely to turn up a profit far in excess of that (in percent) made by a businessman. The IRS is happy about this, of course, and probably pats itself on its corporate back for having the wisdom to go along with the promising beginner in his desperate years.

11

Let The Tips Fall Where They May

(A catch-all collection of tips—
some useful, some not so useful,
but all with a certain value)

CREDIT WHERE IT IS DUE

The thanks that you give people for helping you put your story together can often be reinforced in print through mention of their names. Such a small and simple thing to do, and yet a thing of value to persons who seldom or never see their names in the paper! For them it becomes an item to be clipped and saved, but for you, the writer-photographer, it is a sort of saving grace expressed in honest acknowledgment that, after all, your piece would not have been as good as it is without them.

The writers of books often carry their gratitude to an extreme, and it is not uncommon to see on the acknowledgments page such a slurry of compliments flowing around as to make one wonder if the author himself had anything at all to do with his book. Everyone is brought into the act including "my loyal friends and colleagues without whom . . ." and "my mother without whom . . ." and "far from least my secretary, Cathy Cathcart, who kept the paperclip box filled, and her assistant, Minny Mandrake, who typed the manuscript and otherwise assisted." The patently phony quality of such effusions of love for everybody carries with it the feeling that the author is meeting a contract—"Cathy, if you will keep the paperclip box filled I will put your name in my book." And, "Minny, if you will type the manuscript and make one clean copy, I will immortalize you in print."

The writer-photographer has neither the reason nor the space to carry on like this; but he does have a reason to slip into print in small space some mention of the chief one or two persons or sources without whose help he could not have produced the article. This can be done in the case of a borrowed photograph, for instance, by a credit line acknowledging the "courtesy of the Chester County Historical Society." In most instances, however, the name of the individual who was instrumental to your success can be worked into the text itself as part of the story. As an example, you might say, "After showing me around the lower floors of the old house, the caretaker, Mrs. George Updike, produced a key from her pocket and said, 'There's something in the attic that you should see.'"

In almost every circumstance in which it is necessary to ask for help from people who are in a position to give it—caretakers, curators, guides, officials, research assistants—that help is gladly and generously given. Although nothing is expected in return, it is common consideration and courtesy on the part of the writer-photographer to mention, if he can, the help given or the person giving it.

THE PAYOFF

In close connection with giving credit when and where due is something I choose to call the payoff. Well aware of its original connotation and relation to illegality, I use it here nonetheless because of its apt and understandable meaning. It has nothing to do with the passing of money.

In the case of our grateful author mentioned above, it is to be hoped that the payoff to both Miss Cathcart and Miss Mandrake consisted of, at least, the presentation of an autographed copy to each of them with an inscription on the flyleaf beginning appropriately, "Without you . . ." With such a reward, the girls are set up for life. But in this case also, many others are credited in the acknowledgments and deserve their payoffs . . . all those helpful colleagues and, of course, mother. Here, the author is in trouble, for with so many to pay and so few copies of his book available to him free (usually 10 copies), he will have to buy copies to give away.

With the writer-photographer, the payoff is quite different and is likely to be rewarding to him as well as to the recipient. I find it a pleasure, for instance, to send a tearsheet of the article (copy torn from the paper or magazine) to those who helped me with source material. In effect, it tells them that you really did publish the article, a fact that in most instances they are not likely to know since the publication in which it appeared may not have come their way. It is in a way proof of your sincerity, and to them is a record of their involvement and justification for their help. Most, if not all, of the institutions that you write about collect and keep any sort of publicity about them and your addition to their collection is gratefully received. I have in my files letters from a number of officials (even state officials), curators and the like expressing their appreciation for what I had done for them. My feeling is that they did more for me—but the pleasure goes both ways, and to send tearsheets to all concerned is a good thing to do. I remember my surprise when revisiting an atomic power plant about which I had written several years before to find a tearsheet of the article prominently displayed in a glass case.

You can get tearsheets of your stories in newspapers in either of two ways—run down to the corner and buy a stack of papers (which is expensive, particularly if it is the *New York Times* Sunday edition) or ask the editor for them. I have done both. A sweet secretary at the *Times* told me once that any time I wanted more, all I had to do was to ask for them.

In the case of magazines, it can also be expensive to buy whole copies. However, the editor will usually send you galley proofs of your story if you ask for them—particularly if you ask in advance of publication.

Another way in which the writer-photographer can make worthwhile payoffs occurs when his subject is an individual. Naturally, you will have taken a number of pictures of him, and naturally he would be pleased to have one, especially if it was published. In such cases, I take care to see that he gets both a tearsheet and an 8 by 10 print. The cost of the print is negligible compared to the pleasure derived on both sides of the transaction.

Making the payoff for help received is to me as much a part of the whole deal as depositing the publication's check in the bank—something that is done as a matter of course. For the writer-photographer in general, it is, I think, a necessary and salutary action to take.

ON KEEPING NOTEBOOKS

If we think of the mind as a computer in which facts are stored, we can think of a notebook as the key to their retrieval. To illustrate this statement, I have just flipped open one of my notebooks to a random page on which the date is January 19, 1969. A notation there reads, "George Weymouth's tunnel." To you these words can mean little—but to me they are the key to memory, and a whole flood of thoughts comes to mind as a result of my eye meeting the words through a chance turning of a page. The words call up nothing for you beyond their individual meanings because the facts and circumstances and impressions that they refer to are not stored in your mind. To settle what might be some curiosity on your part, here's what my retrieval system brings to mind about Weymouth's tunnel.

The note was written three years ago, but before, and since then periodic efforts were made to bring small industry into the unspoiled countryside around Chadds Ford. George Weymouth, an interested member of the community and a devotee of the horse and carriage, suggested to friends, probably half in jest and half in wishful thinking, that a tunnel be built under the area to carry automobile traffic across the valley. This is the gist of what the notation refers to, but it evokes a great deal more, including the person who told me about it and the circumstances of its telling. In a few moments, the entire matter will have sunk back into my subconsciousness to be recalled again in exactly the same way whenever I see the same notation in my notebook.

It will be plain, therefore, that the habit of keeping notebooks is worth cultivating. For me, as I think they will be for you, their value is various. A key word or two can be relied upon to bring back whole stories or they can serve as a check on facts or information or they can suggest to you ideas worth developing from their long dormant state. Without these keys you would soon forget all of that material in your head, and would have no reason to recall it.

I said earlier in this book that a writer-photographer need never be without story-ideas to work on. If you have a curious and alert mind that is open to suggestion, you will pick up thoughts wherever you go. If one of them seems worthwhile, a word or two or a line or two in your notebook will preserve them for future use, and in the meanwhile you can afford to go about your present business without trying to remember them. One look in the book recalls them all.

When I say notebook, I do not mean journal or diary, and when I say keeping notes, I do not mean writing reams on a daily basis of events and thoughts and doings. This is not to say that keeping a journal (as the phrase is) is not a good thing to do if you are inclined that way, but for me it would be more like the journal or diary keeping me—too demanding, too full of compulsion, too much an end in itself. To the contrary, notekeeping is an occasional thing done when you are stirred into doing it—undemanding, without compulsion, a means to an end.

I think that the kind of notebook you keep is worth comment. I've tried them all and have settled once and for all on one kind—a stenographer's notebook, the narrower kind that fits into the pocket of a jacket. It has many virtues. Its size is practical and convenient. You can find support for your writing hand, which the small address-type of book will not give you. You can rip out a page from its spiral binding if you like, and never miss it. You can spread it open and stand it on its edges to look at as you type. It is not bulky and cumbersome as a ring-bound or looseleaf job is. It does not present the awkwardness of the spring-bound book. You can't beat it for utility, and when you have filled its pages you can get another just like it at any stationery store.

Keeping a notebook such as this need not be a way of life—but a way of work. If you should find yourself with a thought to record and no notebook to record it in, a condition that greets me from time to time for I do not carry my notebook with me as a regular thing, simply jot down the thought on anything you have with you and transfer it to your notebook later.

In the course of years, you will accumulate notebooks and now and then you will browse through one of them. At least two things will astonish you. One is concerned with your computer and the other with your failure to act. With respect to the computer, you will marvel at the picture it conjures up for you—a long dead thought brought to full life by a scribbled notation placed in your notebook 10 years ago. Your failure to act will be brought instantly to mind when you see a note about a story-idea that remains no more than that. You've been too busy to handle it. But how much better all those years to have had more than you could handle, rather than to have notebooks without a thought in them!

THE CAMERA SEES MORE THAN YOU DO

The eye is one of the most fallible of organs—learn to overcome its faults if you wish to become a seeing photographer. People look at things without seeing them, and then explain the oversight by saying, "I didn't notice it." The eye, whether mechanically perfect or not, seems not to take note of the details within its field of view unless it is ordered to do so by its owner. Its tieup to the mind to which it feeds impressions

Birds and rocks and garbage cans—a typical misuse of the view-finder. The lens always sees all.

The chapel at the Air Force Academy soars to the sky—but the pickup truck anchors it firmly to the ground. The camera saw what the eye ignored—a pictorial goof.

is unlike the connection of the camera lens to the film. The mind, it seems, records what it wants to—the camera records what is in front of it. All you are likely to remember of the total scene at the time you pressed the button is the object you focused on. The camera, on the other hand, saw and recorded every last detail. This is why it is a common experience when looking at prints just back from the photofinisher to realize, for example, that when you were taking a picture of Aunt Mary sitting at her desk you were also taking a picture of the wart on her nose, the rose growing out of her neck, the chewing gum wrapper on the desk, the half empty glass near her hand and the cigarette butt leaning against the ash tray. Aunt Mary was never quite like that—but you saw the picture one way and the camera saw it as it really was. When looking through your viewfinder, your eye failed to record what was there to be seen, but the good, old camera did the job it was made to do. In actuality, your eye was not at fault, but your perception was. You simply did not let your eye transmit to your mind what was there to be seen.

The degree of difference between two photographers using the same equipment, with respect to the quality of the pictures they take, depends upon relative ability to perceive or "to take in with the mind." Accordingly, to make pictures to your fullest ability, knowing that the camera records what it sees, you must do more than see the picture—you must perceive it.

You will have graduated from the ranks of the snapshooter at the moment you look through your viewfinder with the intent to study the details presented to you within the confines of the film frame. The frame does for you what the movie director or artist does for himself when he makes a frame with his hands in estimating a picture possibility—it concentrates the picture, eliminating unwanted and unnecessary areas. As you look through the viewfinder in a practice session, move the camera slowly and deliberately from one side to the other and up and down. Note how the movement changes the picture —note how one scene has in it less clutter and fewer disturbing

This is what happens when you use the wrong lens hood or shade. In this case, a 50mm hood was used on a 28mm lens. The fault could have been corrected in time if more attention had been paid to viewing through the finder.

elements to detract from the wanted picture, or that another suits your intent better when viewed from a lower or higher angle. Most of all, note with great objectivity all of those little details that are there when you look for them. If you had done this when taking Aunt Mary's picture, you would have softened the wart on her nose by paying proper attention to depth-of-field and by avoiding the very sharp picture, and you would have framed the scene to eliminate the other undesirable items or have physically removed them in advance of shooting.

More than once, I have looked at a picture and been surprised by a detail in it of which I had no realization at all at the time I took the picture. The most memorable is a shot of a fisherman's shack on Cape Hatteras, in the print of which appears a wooden duck nailed to the ridge of the roof. I was happy to see the duck, for it is a nice detail, but I had no recollection of seeing it perched there when I composed the picture. This experience may have been the start of my own efforts to see what the camera sees. I realized well enough that most unseen details are likely to be unwanted.

"Next time, don't scratch the negative!"

ON FILING NEGATIVES

As you accumulate negatives and contact sheets, you will need to store them so that you can find them again in a hurry. It is frustrating to know that you have such and such a negative somewhere, to need to make a print of it, and to waste hours trying to locate it. Although commercial filing systems are available, I have found none more practical than that used by an old pro friend, which I adopted for my own use. It consists of a three-ring, looseleaf notebook, some 3 by 5 file cards and a box to hold them, and a bunch of number 10 envelopes. I paste the contact sheet to a sheet of white paper and put it in the ring binder. At the upper right, I number the sheet consecutively, and at the left identify the subject and date it. You will recall that the contact sheet is a single print showing in actual frame size each of the pictures on a roll of 35mm film. It is a great aid in selecting a picture for enlargement, and in identifying a picture that you are looking for. The other way is less practical and takes much more time, for you have to examine the negative film strips one by one by holding them to the light.

The second step in the filing process is to place the subject title of the contact sheet and its number on the small card and file it alphabetically. In this way you accumulate an easy-to-find list of subjects and corresponding number identifications.

The third step is to place the strips of negatives, cut into four strips of five frames each, into the envelope on which you indicate the same number as that on the card and the sheet in the ring binder. You would then file the envelopes by consecutive number. You should place two additional bits of useful information on the envelope also—the kind of film that was

One instance in which an unnoticed detail in the viewfinder added to rather than detracted from the picture. The wooden duck nailed to the roof of this fisherman's shack surprised me when I saw the finished print.

used (Plus-X or Tri-X or whatever) and the ASA speed rating at which the picture was taken (125 or 400 or whatever).

With this system you can find any given negative in a few seconds. Let us say that the subject is Fortress Louisbourg. You would check the alphabetical file card which gives you the number 24. By turning to page 24 in your ring binder, you see contact prints of all 20 frames. You select the number of the frame you want for enlargement, and take the film strip containing it from envelope number 24.

Of course, you can expand upon this system if you need to by categorizing pictures in addition to identifying them individually by subject. For example, if you have a lot of pictures of animals, your file card would carry the number of each set of negatives in which an animal picture is included, and you would then check each number to find what you wanted. However, it is not likely that you will need recourse to such expansion unless you take pictures practically every day, or until you have grown old and gray as a writer-photographer.

There is only one disturbing element to the efficacy of a filing system like this one, or for that matter any filing system, which is the decision to put off the filing chore for a later, more convenient time. For a busy person, a later time exists, but not a more convenient one; and the consequence is a mounting pile of unfiled material which has to be dealt with eventually. Plainly, the better way is to do the job as soon as you have it back from the photofinisher—it takes only a minute or two.

DEVELOPING WRITING DISCIPLINE—ONE WAY

It's been said that the way to write is—to write. There is truth in it, but to do it is harder than it sounds. Many a good writer has stared uncomfortably long at the blank page in his typewriter and given up for the day. One of them is on record as having replaced the page he'd looked at so long because he felt that it "didn't want to be written on." All of us are familiar with the typical image of the frustrated beginning author whose waste basket overflows with crumpled balls of rejected paper.

But despite all this, things do get written—articles, stories, books, plays, fiction, non-fiction, poetry—in an unending stream, a literary production that must depend on some sort of method and discipline. The individual writer has to develop his own system, the way that suits his personal inclination, the way that works for him. Some writers work best in early morning, others accomplish more at night. Some need, or think they need, solitude and absolute quiet, others can write (and be alone at it) in a subway train or boiler room. Only two days ago as this is written, I saw at a clothesline art show a young man banging away at a typewriter held on his knees while hundreds of people jostled along beside him. His concentration was superb, his mind impervious to all but the words flowing onto the page. Evidently, he had decided for himself somewhere along his way that if he was to get it done at all he would have to write when and where he could. This is what we all have to do, especially as freelancers. If you have something to say, you will write it down in spite of false or stuttering starts, but you will do it more quickly and arrive at your own successful system in due time by understanding the pitfalls and avoiding them.

My experience in more than forty years of writing is pertinent. Perhaps you can draw something useful from it. Before I settled down to the kind of discipline required to meet deadlines, I was like almost every other beginner. I put a clean sheet in the machine very neatly, and then thought it important to sharpen a few pencils, arrange a stack of fresh paper for easy reaching and otherwise square myself away for the attack. What an attack! Feeble and floundering and foolish! I wasted hours getting nowhere and then backed off with the notion that the time or the mood or the place was wrong, and that next time would be better. I was waiting for inspiration—mistake number one.

When finally I had something to say, my trouble seemed to

be that I wrote a dozen variations of the opening sentence in my head before putting a word to paper, and then I couldn't decide which avenue to take. That was mistake number two. And two are enough for the moment.

Those who wait for inspiration do not write, and those who write opening sentences in their heads get nothing down on paper. As a consequence of recognizing these facts, a writer can sit down to his typewriter and begin working at will—any day and any time. All he really needs is his material and some idea of what he wants to do with it. Once he begins, the rest follows as though by design—he is writing. And, sometimes it is hard to stop.

Discipline in my case began with the necessity to meet a magazine deadline every two weeks—26 articles a year. I did it for eight years. After the first few deadlines had been met successfully, I never spent another minute wondering if I could meet the next one. I knew that I could. The following 15 years found me writing copy in advertising agency work, an ideal situation in which to develop writing discipline in that the copywriter is limited both by time and by space with no chance to fool around with either. Even with the rigid requirements of schedules, and quite often with unexpected demands for pieces of copy, I cannot recall that I ever sat down to my work in the morning with anything but a feeling of confidence in my ability to do what I had to do that day.

Those copywriting years began with 1943 and ever since then there has seldom been a week in which I missed doing some writing of my own in spare time. I had long since put out of my mind (for it is mental) the thought that I might not be able to produce some writing when I sat down to it. For me, the ability to produce on demand has always been

A million dollar art museum emerges from a derelict, Civil War gristmill on the banks of the Brandywine at Chadds Ford, Pennsylvania. Before and after pictures almost invariably form the basis for a good story.

aided, abetted and compounded by a desire to write, an enthusiasm for my subject, and, not least, the knowledge that I
could make money at it.

The discipline needed has been for many years an acquired
habit and is no longer even thought of, even in connection
with anything as long as a book with its requirement of sus-
tained writing.

"Here lyeth ye body of John Bitsland who departed this . . ." The unfinished inscription on this pre-colonial gravestone raises a question in the curious mind, not about the deceased, but about the stone carver who left the job unfinished. Was he paid for only ten words? Did he die on the job? What? This stone and others in an old graveyard made an interesting feature article.

My way of getting things done is peculiar to me and my circumstances. I was raised on a farm and learned early in life to like getting up at six in the morning. I still do, and by seven I'm at my desk ready to write. By noon or one o'clock, I've put in five or six productive hours. For me, the law of diminishing returns sets in for creative work by afternoon, and

I turn to something physical such as gardening or lawn mowing or walking or bicycling. This seems to set me up properly for another go at it in the evening, and I may work at the typewriter or with an editing pencil for an hour or two. Working like this on Saturdays and Sundays and two or three evenings during the week (after caring for my regular job), I manage to turn out between 3,000 and 4,000 words each week when the project demands it. On short pieces of a thousand or two words, I usually spend a weekend getting the material together and another weekend writing the article.

Lest the reader conclude from this explanation that I must be the complete drudge, dedicated to the typewriter, I hasten to disabuse him. There is a deal of truth in the Roman saying, *Labor Ipse Voluptas* (Work in Itself Is a Pleasure). However there are other forms of voluptas and I am acquainted with some of them. In actuality, I do not work every week as described above. I feel that it is possible and rewarding to work as a writer-photographer in *some* of my spare time, but that I would lose much of my pleasure in it if I made it into a second vocation by devoting to it *all* of my spare time. This would be no more than moonlighting. In fact, I have had the extreme pleasure on occasion of turning down proffered writing jobs that would have paid well in money but not in satisfaction.

In connection with writing discipline and habits, I believe that the writer must train himself to be able to turn out work (such as an assignment having a deadline or some urgency) on demand. On the other hand, if, as a freelancer, he is caught up in it to the extent that he gives it all of his spare time, he will become a perfunctory writer, losing spontaneity and sparkle which spring from enthusiasm. Much is to be drawn from the fallow period between any two enthusiasms. No writer can sustain a peak for long.

Don't Get Mad at the Editor—Unless . . .

It is inevitable in writing and photographing for publication that you will have some sort of contact or dealings with the editor or his assistants. It is equally inevitable that you will not always like what the editor does with your work, and that you will be torn between telling him what you think of him and grinning and bearing it. Whenever possible, choose the latter course because it's the better one for you. But, if an editor's action is intolerable to you there is no law that says you must sit back stupidly and take it. Hit him between the eyes with your criticism. You have lost his publication as an outlet for your work, but you have saved your integrity.

In making the choice between keeping quiet or speaking up, try to consider the editor's problems and how they affect his decisions. He has two main purposes in life—one is to provide good material for his readers, and the other is to leave enough space for his advertisers. Between the demands of the two, he has to give a little and take a little, which is to say that he gives more space to the advertising and takes it away from your article. In doing this he may have to cut your copy 40 or 50 words or drop one of the three pictures he intended to use. But, no matter what he does to accommodate your story and pictures to the space available, you are not going to like it.

If, on reflection, you believe that the editor did not really hurt the story although he cut out some of your most sparkling lines, then let it pass with thanks that he was able to run the story at all. You will gain by it. As you deal more and more with editors and their staffs you will run into the foibles that make them human. You make mistakes and so do they. Most of their mistakes don't amount to much and don't hurt you; but when they do put a foot in it, it is likely to be so heavily done as to make you come out fighting. Most mistakes worth fighting over are concerned with editing that changes the writer's words in such a way as to make him look foolish or incompetent. When an editor or assistant cuts out words in an effort to shorten a piece, and pays no attention to what their loss does to sense or continuity—then the writer should rise up and smite. After all, his name is on the article. This is his work, and when the reader runs into the bad part he will have a poor opinion of the man whose name is on the piece—and never give a thought to the editor who did the dirty work.

In all of my experience with editors I have been able to ride along with the little punches handed out to me—and no harm done. I don't think I'll ever forget the one time when I found it necessary to tell the editor what I thought of him. I wrote him a letter, using 350 choice words selected from the vocabulary of elemental English so that he would understand my meaning. I guess he did—I never heard from him again. I think that other writers and readers must have complained also about this editor's inadequacies, for he disappeared from the scene soon after the incident.

What hurt me to the quick was his cavalier disregard of the truth of my statements in the article. The story was about the differences between roses grown in the greenhouse (the kind you buy at the florist's shop) and those grown in the fields (the kind you grow in your garden). The editor of the magazine, which is one of the most prestigious in the field of horticulture, asked me to write the article, knowing that I had some expertise in the subject. He wanted no more than 900 words and I gave him 870. There was no need to cut the piece—but he did it, and in such a way that he had me saying things that were not true. Here's an example of this: I had said that the greenhouse rose does not do well in the garden, using the phrase "comes a cropper" meaning to fall flat on its face; he changed this (because he was ignorant of the phrase) to "becomes a cropper" which means produces a good crop in the garden.

I almost got a laugh out of reading one change he made which is best exemplified by the following classic sample of misplaced modifiers . . . the man was pushing the baby carriage with a big, fat cigar. But when, as I read on, I found that he had deleted a reference I had made to a person, which made the following paragraph meaningless, my anger overrode all else and I let him know of it.

So I say—recognize the fallibility of editorial people and go

along with it when you can, but don't be a patsy for an incompetent if you should happen to run across one. Your reputation is at stake.

THE "GAG SHOT"

A gag shot is a picture taken as a gag—a fun shot—and is
submitted along with the other photographs that go with a
story. My first experience with a gag shot involved me as the
subject of the picture. The photographer was Jack Rosen who
was assigned by the editor of the *Philadelphia Bulletin* Sunday
magazine to cover a story with me. After he had taken his
pictures and I had collected the information I needed to write
the story, we had a few minutes to spare before going our separate ways. It happened that we were standing near an old,
broken-down frame building. The door was ajar and hanging
by a single hinge. A window with broken panes of glass interested Jack and he said, "Let's make a gag shot. Bergie might
take it." Bergie is B. A. Bergman, a former editor of the *New
Yorker* who had been hired by the *Bulletin* some years before
to establish the Sunday magazine. Jack explained to me what
a gag shot was, then asked me to step into the old building and
look out through the broken glass. He got the picture, and
Bergie used it in the magazine in a column devoted to thumbnail sketches of the magazine's contributors. Bergie gave the
picture to me, and it is reproduced here as a sample of a gag
shot.

I think that a gag shot should spring from the time and the
place if it is to have the quality of believability, and that it
should not be preconceived as an end in itself. Accordingly,
it is not often possible to come up with a good one, which is,
of course, the only worthwhile kind. I have the feeling that
Jack Rosen, who has a marvelous photographic eye, framed my
face with broken glass because he saw in the composition something that reminded him of Grant Wood's tale-telling painting
called *American Gothic*, something forbidding, uncompromis-
ing, and narrow. It is, of course, not the real me.

A good example of a "gag shot," taken by Jack Rosen who was on assignment with me for the *Philadelphia Bulletin*. The face in the window is mine.

Lost Opportunities

Much as the fisherman likes to talk of the one that got away, the writer-photographer (more particularly the photographer part of him) likes to moan about the opportunity that he failed to take advantage of. It happens to the best of photographers now and then, and to the lesser ones as a matter of course. It boils down to the fact that without a camera, a man is not a photographer.

I learned most about this from a single experience years ago while on a vacation trip to the Great Smokies. I had heard about an isolated mountain valley called Cades Cove and wanted to see the place. A "cove" in those mountains is a pocket in the hills, a cup scooped out of the mountain top, a valley at a high elevation. Cades Cove, it seems, was something special and I was lured to the place by its curious history. The cove is about three miles long and a mile wide, and lies tucked away out of sight a few miles out of and above Gatlinburg, Tennessee. The place is now an historic site, but when I first went there it was in much the same condition as when a hundred farm families lived there following the American Revolution and until after the Civil War. During that time, the only access to this remote place and its self-sufficient people was a mountain trail. It is not surprising to learn that the Cades Cove people were unaware of the Civil War until it was almost over.

What surprised me and my wife, however, was actually to see a remnant of the Civil War left untouched there since 1865. The gravel road had led us past a church and a graveyard, and we then stopped to investigate a ramshackle cabin. The walls were lined with newspapers. We were astounded to note on close examination that many of the papers were dated 1865. The headline of one of them announced the death of Lincoln on April 14. Someone from Cades Cove had nailed those papers to the wall to keep the wind out, soon after the War was over. They had been there for 85 years. I attempted to remove the page with the headline about Lincoln, but it crumbled under my fingers. The camera I had then could not record the scene inside the gloomy cabin. It was a bellows-type Kodak without flash and with a slow lens.

When I returned to Cades Cove some seven or eight years later, I was ready for anything photographic, but progress had reached the Cove by then. As an historic site, it had been cleaned up. The cabin was gone.

If this story has a moral in it for the writer-photographer, it is this: if you set out to shoot a bear, take along something more powerful than a peashooter.

The Cades Cove affair was the first milestone in my own progress as a photographer. The newspaper on the wall was the crux of the story and I was not able to get the picture. Since then I have always been ready with the right tools to do the job, which is not the same as saying that I always come home with the picture I want. The most recent of these fluffs occurred earlier this year when by luck I found myself along the Big Sur coast of California. Since it was a business trip, I took with me only the barest equipment for picture-taking— the camera in its carrying case, loaded with Tri-X. The lens was a medium wide-angle (28mm), a good choice for many shooting conditions. By the time I'd reached Big Sur I had managed to get a few pictures and everything was working fine. Then, with dozens of dramatically beautiful scenes all around, the batteries in the light metering system went dead—the Nikon had run out of gas. Whose fault is it when a car runs out of gas? The batteries had been operating for two years—I never gave them a thought.

It was the next day and 150 miles later before I could replace the batteries. The dealer at the Japanese Center in San Francisco said, "Mister, a battery will never run out of juice if you don't let it. You should get new ones every year."

Of course, it is not always possible to prevent a lost opportunity by being diligent in maintenance and ready for anything. Sometimes, in spite of all that you do or can do, something can go wrong at the wrong moment. However, the chances are 99 to 1 that when you and your camera miss out, the fault will be yours.

On Handling the Camera Without Fumbling

As a writer who has handled a typewriter automatically for years, I can rattle along at a great rate without making many errors. Although I use all ten fingers and the touch system, I immediately run afoul of my instincts as soon as I let my glance wander to the keyboard. Then, my speed goes down and my errors go up. The same fumbling will occur with a camera until and unless the photographer learns a few instinctual moves. There are five such moves, and to develop the habit of making them in the same sequence will increase your speed and efficiency in taking pictures.

With the 35mm camera and with other adjustable cameras, the five necessary moves concern the aperture or opening of the lens, the speed of the shutter, focusing the lens, advancing the film (which also cocks the shutter) and pressing the button to release the shutter. Physically and mechanically, it does not matter which of the first four steps is taken first. If you like, you can focus first, or advance the shutter first, and so on—but you cannot release the shutter (take the picture) first, unless, of course, you don't care about the result. To refine this a little more, you can't get the picture at all until you advance the film and thus cock the shutter. Why then is it wise to adopt and follow a set sequence? Simple. Unless you do follow a system, you will sooner or later forget to focus or to use the right aperture or speed. Any of these lapses will result in a bad picture. Apart from the possibility of omitting a necessary step, you will become more efficient in handling the camera with respect to the time available for the shot and the time taken.

The five moves, as I follow them in order, are aperture, speed, focus, film advance and shutter release. You can follow this or one of your own choosing, but be consistent about it. It is wise, I think, to begin with aperture because, after studying the subject, you must decide what depth-of-field characteristics you want in the picture, and the aperture of the lens determines this. When the selection of opening has been made, you must choose the speed which will, in conjunction with the opening, admit the right amount of light for proper exposure. Next, with opening and speed determined, you bring the picture into focus, advance the film and shoot.

When you have settled on your own system and it has become habitual, you will, in effect, be handling your camera with the same easy skill with which the typist turns out error-less copy. Perhaps, the point can be drilled home more force-fully by comparing the camera-handling habit with the habit on which the skilled driver of a stick-shift car depends to put him in command of brake pedal, gas pedal, four gears forward and one reverse—all managed by feet and hand without con-scious thought.

THE FAD WORDS

The Oxford Universal Dictionary defines "fad" as "a crotchety notion, a craze." Since fad words worm their way into the language, live their brief and ugly lives, and then dis-appear mercifully into the past, it seems to be the better part of wisdom for the intelligent writer not to associate himself with them at all. It is easy to recognize the fad word, for it has about it a sorethumb quality that makes it stick out of the page, and a strange newness that clamors for attention. It sticks in your craw for a moment and is hard to swallow. You stop to wonder about it.

Such words pop up regularly and are likely to be seen first in the speeches of politicians and the writings of educators, advertising men and the like who have little grounding in the language and less taste for it. Since they have no regard for bastardization, they plunge into the making of fad words with all the skill and the will of the rapist.

In this way we were given the word "know-how" during the second World War. Not a single manufacturer or indus-trialist could have gotten through the war without it. They all had it, as their advertising people said, and it was an essential ingredient in winning the war. When the war ended, they didn't need it anymore and "know-how" disappeared.

In the years between the war and the present, someone dis-covered the suffix, "ize," and used it to "finalize" a meeting or a report or a decision and the semi-literate world had some-thing new to hold on to for a while. They tacked it on many a worthy adjective and made a worthless verb. "Ize" seems now to have run its feverish course and is gone.

Instead, we have "meaningful" words and statements that help us "extrapolate" our thoughts and deductions and arrange them into useful "parameters." How *did* we ever manage before? Are you one of those, "hopefully," who looks forward to the day when you will no longer see in print such words as "charisma," which no personality seems to be without, and "chauvinist," which apparently all male pigs seem to be?

Do not be gullible. Fad words will be around as long as an empty mind exists to spawn them, and as long as there is space on the page to insert them. Monkey see, monkey do.

ESTIMATING NUMBER OF WORDS

Every writer seems to have his own way. For anything under five manuscript pages in length, I count the words in the first five lines, get the average per line and multiply by the number of lines. For anything between five and fifteen pages, I count the words on a page and multiply by number of pages. For anything above that, I count the words on the first five pages, get the average per page and multiply by the number of pages.

Estimates like these are accurate enough and seem to satisfy the needs of editors with whom I have worked. Since some low-pay publications pay by the word, it would be smart in dealing with them to count every word.

TITLE, HEADLINE, CAPTION AND LEGEND

The ancient philosophers used to define their terms before letting the argument begin so that when a given term was used each participant would know what the other meant by it. Confusion exists in many fields when a lax approach to the use of terms is permitted, the result being misunderstanding and actual errors in the work itself.

In the field of publishing, including newspapers, magazines and books, three terms—title, headline and caption—are often interchanged and their finer meanings lost, and a fourth—legend—is now seldom used at all. To be literal about them, a title is the name of a thing or what it is called; a headline is that and nothing more, the line at the head of a printed piece; a caption is a heading of some sort, too, and appears to be (as it is generally used) something of a cross between headline and title; a legend, properly used, describes, identifies or tells the story of an illustration, or identifies a set of keys or symbols.

Insofar as the writer-photographer is concerned, most of this is academic. However, your editor might let you know that you forgot to submit captions with your photographs, in which case he really means legends.

How to Overcome Camera Shake

Imperceptible as it may be, there is movement of your camera whenever you take a picture. It is impossible to hold a camera in your hands so that it is totally still. Even when a camera seems to be solidly held on a sturdy tripod, it is subject to vibration through the ground or floor. But for all intents and purposes, these movements are overcome by one means or another and you get pictures that do not reveal camera shake. Without such means, a picture tends to exhibit a kind of fuzziness which you might mistake for poor focusing.

You will recall from your study of physics that with every action there is an equal and opposite reaction. Quite apart from the movements of your body is the movement caused by such reaction. For instance, when you press the button to release the shutter, which is under spring tension, reaction movement occurs, and in the case of cameras with flip-up mirrors there is further movement as the mirror flips up and returns to its position. All of the mechanical movements within the camera contribute to the total movement.

Even so, all such movement is effectively and practically dispensed with when you use a sufficiently fast speed in exposing the film and at the same time take precautions to hand-hold the camera as firmly as possible. Obviously, you must use greater care in holding the camera when you are using the slower speeds and when you are shooting with a long lens. In the latter instance, the longer the lens, the greater the tendency to movement. It is generally agreed among professional photographers that a 135mm lens can be hand-held successfully at a shutter speed of $\frac{1}{60}$ second; and a few seem to be able to do it at $\frac{1}{30}$. In order to accomplish this, they resort to all sorts of methods which can be applied in your own work when you are using any length of lens and the lower shutter speeds.

The trick is to brace yourself as best you can and to hold the camera firmly against your nose and forehead. Your elbows can be brought tight to your chest. Lean against a wall or other solid object if possible. Hold your breath at the moment of releasing the shutter. Let the strap around your neck come to your aid—with a little trying you can put your left arm through it, taking up the slack and providing support. Riflemen use a similar tactic to steady their guns. If your camera is equipped with an automatic timing lever, you can use it to advantage by setting the timer at three to six seconds, aiming the camera, pressing the shutter release button—and then concentrating on holding the camera steady until the timer releases the shutter. In this way, you avoid completely any movement caused by pressing the button.

As you experiment, you may come up with still other methods to avoid camera shake. But whatever system you devise, always keep in mind that the release button should never be jabbed at or punched. Exert steady pressure on it. As in the case of the rifleman—"squeeze" off your shot.

PLAGIARISM AND HOW TO AVOID IT

Plagiarism is defined as the using, taking, borrowing (stealing) of someone else's idea or material and presenting it as one's own. There are laws against it—but the most potent force militating against it lies within the writer-photographer's conscience and his sense of the fitness of things.

It is senseless to consider here the deliberate plagiarization of another's work. The self-respecting writer won't do it. It is quite another matter, however, to consider how one might slip into a little lifting here and there through careless working habits and unconscious or unthinking action. It begins, or is most likely to begin, with the writer's source material.

Let us say, for instance, that you research a given subject that you intend to write about. You talk to people, you collect printed pieces about it, you read its history in the encyclopedia. You have the facts and your own impressions. Somewhere along in the writing of your piece you check a fact in one of the printed sources and before you know it you have picked up word for word the sentence or the paragraph concerning the fact. It seems like a small thing, but it is the easy way and before you know it you are lifting another set of someone else's words. This is plagiarism in a small way—but it has a way of growing bigger.

You can avoid it altogether and prevent its becoming a habit to lean on by never picking up a single unquoted sentence as it stands in a printed piece. The facts are all you need and the facts are open to everybody to use, but it is up to the writer to use them in his own words and sentence structure.

I recognized long ago the danger of falling into the pit of plagiarism through inadvertence. As a consequence, I religiously set aside all of my source material when I have once digested the facts, and go back to check them only after I have completed the writing.

Fair Use and the Public Domain

When a writer is considering the use of printed material copyrighted by some other author, writer or publication, he is governed by several conditions, among them whether the material is still under copyright protection or is in the public domain, and whether his use of it falls into the area of fair use.

The copyright laws of this country protect material for an initial period of 28 years after which the holder of the copyright can renew it for another similar period. If the original copyright is not renewed, and when the 56 year period expires, the protected material loses its protection and is in the public domain, in which case it is free to all.

To quote or excerpt from copyrighted material, the writer or author must obtain permission from the copyright holder if the material that he wants to use is fairly extensive. If he uses such material as his own and without permission he is open to a law suit. The principle of fair use, on the other hand, permits reasonable use of copyrighted material without permission. Falling within this sphere would be occasional short quotations or excerpts used to make a point or illustrate the matter under consideration, all duly credited as to source.

However, there is the possibility, when a writer is using copyrighted material under his idea of what the fair use principle is, that he may go too far and pick up substantial material —too much in the view of the copyright owner who is then likely to sue. The law itself does not define what is reasonable and unreasonable—what is small, enough or too much. It is entirely up to the writer himself to decide if the material he has used lies within fair use. This can put too great a burden on judgment, and when the matter seems doubtful, the best course is to get permission or not to use the material.

OUTLINE IT—THEN WRITE IT

One of the most useful courses that I ever took in school, as I look back on it, was not something offered in a college curriculum but one that was forced on me by a grammar school teacher. She believed that the way to an understanding of the construction of written English was to tear each sentence apart and to examine each word to see what part it had to play in the sentence. We dissected the sentence, diagrammed it on the blackboard, parsed it from end to end. In this way, we learned to construct a sentence, too, and then went on to the paragraph and the final story.

Out of these basics, I learned to believe in the value of an outline when writing longer pieces—the skeleton on which to arrange the flesh of the story—the armature on which to plaster the putty of the statue—the roadmap to guide you to your destination. The shorter pieces are easy to handle when attention is paid to beginning, middle and end; but the longer ones present a problem of a different sort. Any writer, working from a mass of material, can find himself going astray, getting off the path and even wandering around in circles like a child lost in the wood, unless he has a compass to guide him. Without something firm to build around, he is likely to find himself in the end with an amorphous blob, a story without form, shape or solidity.

Working without an outline leads to repetition of thought, statement or word. What was said 3,000 words earlier can be forgotten, and reiterated. What was meant to be said at a given point in the article is not remembered and is lost. Apart from the value of an outline as a guide to logical flow is another value provided by it which pays off in time and money. This value takes the stuttering out of your progress—it lets the work proceed according to plan and without delay caused by floundering about in search of the next thing to say. I sometimes spend more time building an outline than writing the story—a course that might serve you. (As a matter of interest, the actual outline on which this book was constructed appears in the Appendix.)

ANATOMY OF A STORY

In Chapter 8 a brief description is given of how it became possible for me to write the story of an R.D. mailman. The story lends itself admirably to dissection in order to see what kind of glue was used to hold it together because it is entirely different in kind from the two stories analyzed in Chapter 5. One of those serves to illustrate the beginning, middle and end, as well as narration and description; the other, somewhat longer piece includes these elements but adds argumentation and makes use of a preamble and a peroration or kind of summing up. The interesting thing about each of these three kinds of story is that its form was dictated by the demands of the material. The story of the Kentucky rifle called mainly for description and narration; the Linchester Mill story required these and the posing of a point of view (argumentation) or the stating of a position. Since the third story, which is reproduced below, is about a man and his job it leans heavily on description, reporting and interpetation, and uses personality, atmosphere and anecdote to create a sympathetic and favorable attitude on the part of the reader. (Curiously, when permission was sought from the Post Office Department to ride with a mailman, officials wanted to know if the tone of the story was to be sympathetic or critical. Permission was granted when they were assured that criticism was not intended.) The story ran in the *Philadelphia Bulletin* Sunday magazine on December 13, 1964—timed beautifully by the editor to evoke kind thoughts about the mailman at Christmastime.

RIDING THE R.D. TRAIL

Since he took on the job of delivering mail 12 years ago to the people of Rural Route 4 out of West Chester, 37-year-old Francis (Franny) Quay has whipped open and slammed shut a total of 1,310,400 mailboxes, and traveled the equivalent of nearly eight times around the world.

He has ridden his route an estimated 3,744 times . . . and yet every day as he starts out he knows that R.D. 4 will produce something new, different and unusual to lighten the humdrum routine.

"I like my people," he told me, "and they seem to like me. I enjoy serving the 410 boxes on my route, and I can't imagine any other job that I'd rather have."

After riding one day with Franny Quay, I couldn't imagine a more perfect melding of man and job. However, Quay doesn't "serve boxes," as he put it—he serves the people behind the boxes and they know and appreciate it. Here in one man they have a mail carrier, a wet nurse, a hired hand, a messenger, a friend in need, and an "uncle" to their children to whom he gives lollypops and sticks of chewing gum.

At Christmastime, he is even more—a working Santa Claus bearing cheerfully his mountainous burden of bales, boxes and bundles, and what seems like a million holiday messages of good will.

"When I deliver a Christmas package," said Franny, "it makes me feel good—like I'm a part of somebody's happiness. Just the same, I wish people would mail earlier than they do. Maybe they would if they realized that the R.D. carrier is the guy at the small end of the funnel. Everything on his route—going and coming—has to pass through his hands. And he has only two of them!"

It was 7:20 A.M. when I reached the Post Office on Gay Street in West Chester to spend a day with Franny on his rounds. Thomas McIntyre, the Postmaster, and Frank Barry, the Superintendent of Mails, offered me the run of the place. A definition of "chaos" could be "an 85-man Post Office between seven and nine in the morning"; but "efficiency" could fit the definition equally well. As I stood bewildered amid the flurry and flow of mail into pigeon holes and yawning canvas bags, of hurtling hand trucks and shouted comments, and wondered how it would all come out, the Postmaster's calm smile assured me that the people of West Chester and environs, all 38,000 of them, would get their mail on time as usual.

If I'd had any doubts about the people on R.D. 4 they would have been allayed on meeting Franny Quay. A sturdily built man of middle height with an open, mobile face, he stood before his sorting case in a small cubicle at the side of the room quietly and confidently thrusting the right mail into the right box.

"I could do this in my sleep," he said, "and still get it ninety five percent right. Sit on the stool there and ask me anything you like. It won't bother me to talk."

Somebody stuck his head in the doorway. "Hey, Franny! Anything the matter? I see you got an Inspector on your trail!"

"Don't mind the boys," Franny said. "If you can't take a ribbing you don't belong in the Post Office. They heard that you were coming today."

By 8:30 Franny had sorted his letters, newspapers and magazines according to the sequence of mailboxes on the route, packaged them into convenient bundles held by straps and loaded them into his 1958 Opel station wagon. "Now we'll run down to the Annex and pick up our Parcel Post packages," Franny said as I climbed into a space he'd left for me on the rear seat. "Then we'll be on our way."

By nine o'clock we were heading for R.D. 4. "This route is 52 miles long and takes about four hours to cover depending on what happens and if everything holds together," Franny said. "The car has 98,000 miles on it and the clutch isn't too good. Got my eye on a four-wheel-drive wagon. Hope to get it soon."

I wanted to know what Franny meant by "depending on what happens."

"Well," he said, "any R.D. carrier in the country will tell you that sometimes his people need help in one way or another—so you give it to them if you can. Who wouldn't? You never can tell what's in a mailbox until you open it. I got a note once that said, 'Dear Franny, please take the blanket off the horse in the barn.' The woman was sick or away for the day—I forget.

"Another time a man way out in the country asked me to feed his sheep while he was on a winter vacation, so I stopped and fed them their grain every day. It didn't take much time. He couldn't have gotten away otherwise."

As we pulled up before the only house in sight on a back road a small tow-headed boy came running to the mailbox. Franny handed him a card. "Give this to your sister (the boy's married sister with whom he'd been living since his mother died). Tell her there's a C.O.D. package at the Post Office. She'll have to pay $116 to get it." The boy rolled his eyes upward, slapped his hand against his forehead in mock consternation and said, "And I know where she'll get the money! Out of my savings account! I've got $300 in it!" Franny told me the C.O.D. package contained glassware.

Down the road we came to a long, winding driveway. Franny turned into it instead of stopping at the mailbox. "I have a package for these people and I owe them a favor so I'll take it to the house and save them a trip down."

"What did they do for you?"

"The other day they let me and my son, he's 9, fish in their pond. Ray caught two dandy bass."

As the morning wore on Franny chipped away at his carload of mail. I had time to notice something about R.D. mailboxes. Although they are supposed to be set with the bottom of the box 38 inches above the ground, some are 48 inches high, and one was actually only 24 inches.

To serve boxes that do not meet government regulations imposes a strain on Franny Quay, for he has to leave the car many times to reach them. He didn't complain about the boxes. "The people have other things on their minds," he said. Some boxes are set on iron "I" beams in Gibraltar-like solidity, some tremble like an aspen leaf in the zephyr air and are held by a dead branch stuck in the ground, some shine bright with new paint, others bear the rust of ages.

We stopped at a rusty box next to which was a newer one. "Watch this!" Franny warned. He opened the rusty box slowly, gingerly. The inside was angry with buzzing bees. He shut it carefully, then put mail in the adjoining box. "I have several like this. They had to be abandoned and new boxes put up. I've found other things besides bees. Once a live chicken scrambled out of one of them; another had a dead possum in it. Somebody playing jokes."

Some of the names on R.D. 4's boxes intrigued me (that is, when there were names), such as Hipp, Hopp, Fling, Ax, Nix. "There's a Bird, a Fox, and a Trout, too," Franny said.

We rounded a corner and came down out of the woods to a farm pasture where the farmer and a couple of boys were trying to corner an enormous Black Angus bull. We stopped to watch and I had the feeling that Franny Quay was about to leap from the car to lend a hand. If he had done so, I would have felt it my duty to remain behind to protect the United States mail. But there was no need and we drove on.

"Has anybody ever complained about your service?" I asked Franny. "Once," he said with a laugh, "I got a call at the Post Office from a woman who was pretty mad at me about a new dress I'd just delivered. I hung the package on the mail box by the cord and her dog got hold of it after I'd left. He ripped the package open and was running all over the place dragging the dress after him. We're supposed to put packages under cover in wet weather, but this was a sunny day. I didn't count on her dog."

Almost suddenly we pulled up at a mailbox with the name "Tanguy" on it. Franny took a paper bag from the box, looked into it and said, "Seckel pears today. She usually leaves peaches." I met Mr. and Mrs. Charles Tanguy, pleasantly sunny-faced people who brightened visibly when they learned that Franny was not breaking in a new man on R.D. 4.

At Chester County Farms (the County prison) the Warden,

Charles Frame, a courteous man, greeted Franny and me, and assured me that I would be welcome at any time. Franny told the
young woman, Mrs. Eileen Burns, to whom he delivered the bag of
mail in the office that he had a package of educational records for
her blind son from the Library of Congress and would deliver it
to her home mailbox. The package was postage free and marked,
"Property of the United States Government."

It was one o'clock when we headed for West Chester, our traveling Post Office carrying back perhaps forty or fifty letters and a
few orders for stamps. "You know," said the Postmaster of R.D. 4
as we skimmed along a hilly, dirt road, "it isn't all one-sided. These
people help me out plenty. When I get stuck in snow or mud, and
it happens often, there's always somebody with a truck or tractor
to pull me out, and the mail gets through."

After stopping for a bowl of soup at a roadside place, we went to
Quay's home on R.D. 1 at the outskirts of northern West Chester
where I met Lois, his wife, and husky, young Ray. The Quays,
whose interests include the Presbyterian Church, have a right to be
proud of their trim, one-story, three-bedroom home which was
built by Franny himself.

"It took me sixteen months to build it. I'd had some experience
with carpentry on construction jobs after I left the Navy in 1950.
I was in for five years serving on a cruiser in the North Atlantic.
Came out a gunner's mate. I left West Chester High School without
finishing the course and worked at various jobs for a couple of
years before joining the Navy."

The pleasant neatness of the Quay home spoke of Lois's prowess
as a homemaker; the three beagles in their backyard pen and the
guns and the deer head on the wall of the spare room told of
Franny's outside interests. "I love the fields and woods and the back
country. That's why I enjoy R.D. 4."

Back at the Post Office, I was congratulated for having survived
R.D. 4 in Franny's Opel. Postmaster McIntyre grinned amiably.
Francis Quay went to work on his time sheet.

I felt that Franny Quay earns and deserves every cent of his
$7,771 annual pay, his hospitalization benefits, his two-week sick
leave each year, his three-week vacation and his right to retire at 55
(as he expects to do) on a solid part of his salary.

I went home with a new understanding of my own R.D. mail

carrier, and a better appreciation of his services performed for me six days a week. Then I went out and checked my mailbox to see if it was 38 inches above the ground.

It will be seen that the first few short paragraphs of the mailman story serve to set the stage for the actual recounting of a day in the life of Franny Quay. They also tend to whet the appetite and arouse the curiosity of the reader so that he will want to continue to read. The idea of building the mailman into something more than a carrier of mail—messenger, hired hand and the like—evokes sympathy and a bit of admiration for him, especially at Christmastime when he becomes a kind of Santa Claus for the children along his route.

With all the props in place and the atmosphere itself created, the main body of the story begins. The mailman sets out as usual to sort and deliver his mail, but he has a reporter riding along to tell what happens. From this point to the end, the story unfolds as the old Opel travels the route, each event following in order and described as it happened. To enliven what might otherwise have been a dull recital, the writer asks questions and records the answers, and brings his own observations into the piece. Thus, a running conversation takes place—the curious names on the mailboxes are noted—interesting anecdotes are brought in. The mailman's problems (carelessly situated mailboxes, mud, snow and rain, an aging car) are delineated. The regard held for the mailman by his "people" comes out in one way or another, and throughout the story his own feelings for the boxholders is evident in many ways.

In the end, the mailman emerges as a solidly dependable character for whom I, myself, felt the pangs of empathy. After all, when I got home I did remember and took the trouble to measure the height of my own mailbox—a fitting end to the story.

Appendix

This is the outline on which *The Writer-Photographer* was based. It is included here for the possible benefit of the reader who would like to compare the bare bones of the book with the fleshed-out form. In making such a comparison, it should be borne in mind that occasional deviations from the outline were made as a new thought or expediency called for them. Nonetheless, the outline was followed in the main, and served to keep the writing on course.

CHAPTER 1
Writing and Photography—A Matched Team

A. Like the words and music of a song—each can stand separately but go best together
B. Skill in the use of one makes the other more valuable
  1. Example—a story might sell for $100 without pictures and bring $200 with them
    a. One skill alone limits income
C. The typewriter is a machine that records thoughts and statements; the camera is a machine that records what it sees
  1. Use them in conjunction to record the whole story
  2. Case History—The *Philadelphia Bulletin* staff photographers and I
D. The camera can save time for the writer
  1. It can copy documents and lengthy descriptions or background facts for later use, thus saving laborious hand copying

2. Example—shooting documents at Fortress Louisbourg and at Cape Hatteras

CHAPTER 2
How to Recognize a Story When You See One

A. Story ideas are always available if your mind is open to receive them
   1. The question of what to write about disappears
B. Most people look at things but do not see them
   1. To see story possibilities in a looked-at subject suggests ways to approach the story
      a. Example—stray dog story
      b. Example—famous steeple story
C. To see a story requires the uses of imagination, curiosity and the association of ideas
   1. One thought inevitably leads to another
   2. Imagination is the extension of what you see or know or have experienced
      a. Stir your imagination by asking yourself questions—how can this be used? What is interesting about this? Who would like to read about this? How shall I approach the story?
D. Story ideas can be developed both from what you see in passing, and what you deliberately look for
   1. What you see in passing occurs by chance
      a. Case History—the Three Trees
   2. What you know predetermines the story
      a. If you know that the anniversary of an historical event is coming up next year you can anticipate it by writing the story now, and the story will be timely. Case History—the Mason-Dixon Line
      b. Rich source of story ideas—reference books such as World Almanac
E. When the well runs dry
   1. You need new enthusiasm, new interest, new impressions
   2. Take a notebook and a camera and go for a ride
      a. It doesn't matter what road you take

    b. Be aware of the passing scene
    3. Two to one you'll come back with a story
F. The camera alone can produce story ideas
    1. Carry your camera everywhere
    2. Take photos first, then weave stories around them
    3. Example—before and after pictures of restored house

CHAPTER 3
How to Research the Story and Gather Material

A. The need for accurate information—the facts and plenty of them
    1. Believability depends on correct information
        a. Readers delight in finding errors of fact and pointing them out in letters to the editor
        b. An incorrect statement leads to distrust of entire piece
    2. The editor's confidence in you depends on your care and thoroughness
        a. If you lose it through inaccuracies you lose sales
        b. Example—Mason-Dixon Line story
B. Sources of story information
    1. The persons interviewed
        a. What they tell you
        b. What they give you in printed form—folders, maps, pictures
        c. Example—1704 House
    2. Local historical societies and their archives
        a. Always glad to help in return for copy of printed piece
        b. Example—taking picture on chair at Chester County Historical Society
    3. Libraries and librarians
    4. Your own reference books
        a. Dictionaries, encyclopedias, biographies, histories, Bartlett's Quotations (a godsend), atlas, gazetteer
    5. Your own detective work
        a. Ask questions—put two and two together
        b. Example—finding George Johnson
C. Get all the facts whether you think you need them or not
D. Learn to form and use impressions of the subject
    1. My method—jotting down key words—writing from a feeling for the subject

E. Important—the way you represent yourself to the person who can help you
   1. Explain who you are and what you want
   2. Do not misrepresent yourself as a staff writer for a publication when you are a freelancer
      a. "Are you the man from the *New York Times?*"—Linchester story

CHAPTER 4
How to Get the Pictures You Need

A. Take the pictures while you are there—act as though you can't come back
   1. You can't go back
      a. Waste of time and money
      b. Distance is often too great
      c. The scene or characters change
      d. The exception—Cornwall Furnace story
B. Take more shots than you are likely to use
   1. Film is cheap
   2. Shoot the scene, the people, the objects from different angles
      a. Pick and choose the ones you'll submit after you've seen them all—contact sheet
   3. Bracket your shots if in doubt about exposure
      a. Shoot at one exposure—then shoot at 1 f/ stop on each side of the first exposure. One will be right
C. Be prepared to handle any condition encountered
   1. Have plenty of film
      a. Cite running out of film in Vancouver and at Cornwall
   2. Take flash equipment along
D. Safety measures
   1. Have a backup camera in case prime camera fails
      a. Cite Corbit House fiasco (slow shutter)
      b. Cite time mirror came loose
      c. A simple instamatic will do in a pinch if you can't afford a second camera
   2. A friend who does photofinishing
      a. Invaluable in case of need
         i. When you need a print in a hurry

     ii. When you need only a small part of the negative enlarged

     iii. When a dense negative can be made into an acceptable print

CHAPTER 5
Writing the Story

A. Consider the subject
  1. What kind of people will be interested in it?
    a. Think about your audience
    b. Adopt a tone or level designed for them—general or specific class of readers
  2. What do your readers want to know about it?
    a. The what, when, where, how, who and why of it
    b. Getting the reader to identify with it
    c. Arousing his interest
  3. Present the facts accurately
B. Consider the story line or theme
  1. Most story-articles are expositions or descriptions
  2. A thread of particular interest should run through the story
    a. Maintains interest and leads to a conclusion
    b. Keeps the story on the track
C. Consider the beginning, the middle and the end
  1. The beginning should arouse interest at once
    a. Throw the first paragraph away
      i. Unless you grab the reader in the first paragraph, you might as well
      ii. There is no time to warm up
    b. Find a peg to hang the story on
      i. Cite opening paragraph of Codorus story
  2. The middle should *be* the story and maintain interest
    a. The meat is in the middle
  3. The end should round out the piece
    a. Draw a conclusion—sum up the story
    b. Leave the reader with an up-note
D. Consider the use of words
  1. The best writing is unobtrusive
    a. Avoid the obscure or sorethumb word

2. A good writer uses enough words—and that's all—to get his meaning across
   a. His reader gets an uncluttered message
3. Prefer the Anglo-Saxon over the Latin-rooted word
   a. It's quicker, less cumbersome
4. Prefer verbs and nouns over the qualifiers
   a. They make the piece run

E. The first draft
   1. Let the words come out on yellow paper
   2. Don't try to write as though this were the final draft
      a. Cross out and change as you go
   3. Let the entire piece gel overnight—then read it cold from beginning to end without stopping to correct
      a. You'll get a fresh look at it and will spot anything wrong
   4. Now go over every word, correcting and rephrasing as needed

F. The final draft
   1. Make additions and changes as you go
      a. New ideas often occur
   2. Check all wording and dates for typographical errors after final typing

G. How many words should you write?
   1. A book or a paragraph can be written on any subject
      a. You must tailor your piece to the need or requirement of the publication whose readership you are after
         i. Study the publications you have in mind
         ii. Does a publication use 1,000–2,000 or more words?
   2. Never write more than necessary to tell the story
      a. Padding a story is phony and obvious

CHAPTER 6
Photography for the Writer—The Camera and Its Uses

A. Introduction to kinds of cameras
   1. A camera is a box having a hole at one end and film at the other
      a. All cameras function on the same principle
      b. Difference lies only in lenses, controls and methods of operation

    2. What kind of camera is best for the writer?
       a. Compare kinds of cameras—instamatic, twin-lens reflex, single-lens reflex, Polaroid

B. Know your camera as well as you do your typewriter
    1. Quality of story and pictures should be equal
    2. Study your camera's functions—know what it can do

C. No camera or lens is best for all picture situations
    1. Camera that uses interchangeable lenses is desirable
    2. Why the SLR above all others?

D. Kinds of lenses
    1. Normal lenses—50mm or 55mm
       a. General purpose work
       b. Usually a fast lens for low light work
    2. Wide-angle lenses—28mm or 35mm
       a. Have greater depth-of-field—less need to focus sharply
       b. For work at close quarters
       c. For broad landscapes
       d. For interiors
    3. Long lenses (telephoto)—85mm or 105mm or 135mm
       a. For bringing a part of a scene closer
       b. For unobtrusive portraiture
       c. For filling the frame

E. Examples of using different lenses for certain effects

F. Kinds of films (black and white) for newspaper and periodical reproduction
    1. Verichrome—its uses
    2. Plus-X—its uses
    3. Tri-X—its uses
    4. ASA speed ratings

G. Pros and cons of having your own darkroom

CHAPTER 7
The Market—And How to Make One Subject Do Double Duty

A. A single subject can lend itself to double treatment—double sales
    1. Same subject—different audience—different approach
       a. Peach Bottom story for N.Y. *Times* and for *Printed Page*
       b. Linchester Mill

2. A newspaper feature can be given in-depth treatment for use in a magazine or house organ
   a. Writing should be entirely new—no two paragraphs the same
   b. Photos should be entirely different
   c. A reason for getting all the information and enough pictures
3. The Codorus story, used in a booklet, would make an ideal subject for a feature magazine article or even a book

B. The voracious maw of the media
1. Must be fed by writer-photographers
2. Market for a story on a given subject opens again a year later
   a. Cite *Times* experience with Corbit House and Fortress Louisbourg articles

CHAPTER 8
How to Know What Editors Want

A. An editor must provide what his publication's readers want to read
1. In a sense, all reader-groups are specialized
   a. General publications appeal to mass readership
      i. Usually unsophisticated, light, casual reading
   b. Trade publications appeal to readers within a given business or industry
   c. Children's publications appeal to children
   d. Literary publications appeal to highly literate readers
2. Knowledge of the class of publication indicates the kind of article accepted
   a. A study of recently published articles in a magazine or newspaper supplement the current trend of acceptance

B. Querying the editor on a story idea—or not
1. A moot point depending on the individual editor
   a. You have to learn to know which is better
   b. "What else have you got for us?" Cite *Times* experience on multiple story suggestions
2. In general, the submitted story complete with pictures has a better chance because it is a fait accompli that can be judged

C. Editors always *do* look for and want to buy good material
  1. When you are accepted, come right back with another story
    a. You may never know or see the editor personally, but your name will register
    b. Cite *Bulletin* exchange of notes between assistant editor and editor

CHAPTER 9
How to Help the Editor to Like Your Work

A. Editors are professionals who like to deal with professionals
  1. You can influence the editor if you act like a pro
B. The professional way to submit your material
  1. List rules for submission of text and photos
C. Never overlook the smallest detail or the largest
  1. Neatness counts
    a. A clean manuscript makes a favorable impression
  2. Thoroughness is the mark of the pro
    a. Spell it right
    b. Punctuate it reasonably
    c. Answer questions before the editor or reader asks them
    d. Using rubber cement, paste typewritten legends on back of photos
    e. Don't make the silly mistake
      i. Pages out of order
      ii. Return postage and envelope not included in package
      iii. A hopeful, or any, covering letter
      iv. Poorly packaged manuscript and photos
      v. Folded materials—staples
D. In general, put yourself in the place of the editor
  1. How would you like to receive material?

CHAPTER 10
The Writer-Photographer and the IRS

A. You are self-employed if you work full time or part time for yourself
  1. In either case, you are entitled to the benefit of tax laws
    a. Know these laws and save money

B. The self-employed are entitled to deduct the costs of producing income

C. Typical deductible costs of the writer-photographer

1. A percentage of costs of maintaining an office in your home
   a. If you have a six-room house and use one room for your work, deduct one-sixth of mortgage or rent payments and of heat and light bills
   b. If you use your home phone for business calls, deduct actual cost of calls and a percentage of monthly phone charges
2. A percentage of costs of your automobile if you use it in gathering material or covering an assigned story, including insurance, maintenance, licenses and gasoline is deductible
3. Entire costs of all supplies needed in work production, including paper, film, film processing, research books, typewriter ribbons, postage
4. Travel expenses—motels, food, tolls—incurred on business trips concerned with writing and photography
5. Depreciation costs of automobile, typewriter, camera equipment

D. Keeping cost records

1. Jot down in a notebook all out of pocket expenses with dates incurred
2. Get and keep receipts for all purchases of size—supplies etc.
3. Figure out at year's end all maintenance expenses for home

E. Employ tax accountant to figure returns

1. Complexities too great to handle with justice to your situation
2. His fee is deductible
3. Give him all your data—income and expense
4. Be prepared to justify your figures

CHAPTER 11
Let the Tips Fall Where They May

A. Credit Where It Is Due
B. The Payoff
C. On Keeping Notebooks
D. The Camera Sees More Than You Do
E. On Filing Negatives

F. Developing Writing Discipline—One Way
G. Don't Get Mad At The Editor—Unless . . .
H. The "Gag Shot"
I. Lost Opportunities
J. On Handling The Camera Without Fumbling
K. The Fad Words
L. Estimating Number of Words
M. Title, Headline, Caption and Legend
N. How To Overcome Camera Shake
O. Plagiarism And How To Avoid It
P. Fair Use And The Public Domain
Q. Outline It—Then Write It
R. Anatomy Of A Story